A MAN FROM MINMI

MY DAD - JOE THOMPSON'S STORY

GEOFFREY THOMPSON

ETT IMPRINT
Exile Bay

Joe Thompson, Balmain, Rawson Cup winners 1911

This edition published by ETT Imprint, Exile Bay 2018

ETT IMPRINT
PO Box R1906

Royal Exchange NSW 1225 Australia

ISBN 978-1-925706-55-0 (ebook)

ISBN 978-1-925706- 53-4 (paper)

The Publisher would like to thank Sandra Roberts, Lesley de Vries and Mary Thom for their help in getting this book to press.

Design by Hanna Gotlieb

CONTENTS

Joe Thompson, Pupil Teacher at Minmi Public School 1906.

MINMI

My Dad, Joseph Walter Thompson, was born on 17th October 1889 at the home of his parents Thomas and Susan, in Railway Street in the coal mining town of Minmi, north of Newcastle in New South Wales.

Dad's mother Susan was the eldest daughter of William Moore who came from Cambridgeshire, England (b. 1812) and Mary English who had emigrated from Tipperary, Ireland (b. 1814). Having an Irish-born grandmother gave Dad what he often referred to as 'the right to call himself an Irishman.' What we did not know until the 1980s was that his grandfather, William had been a convict, having been sentenced in August 1829 (in Cambridgeshire) to 14 years imprisonment on one (only) charge of housebreaking. His arrival in New South Wales followed his transportation in the convict sailing ship *Adrian* in December 1830 and he was assigned to the Church of England Manse at the Hunter River. He was recorded at the time of his sentencing as being 5 feet 5½ inches in height, with blue eyes, and his occupation listed as 'Shoemaker - Perfect'. On 30th April 1840 he was granted the status of 'Ticket of Leave'.

Apparently it was in the Hunter River district that he met Mary English, who had arrived at Sydney as a Free Settler in the sailing ship

Alfred on 16th January 1839; being of that status, only her occupation as 'Dairymaid' and her religion as Roman Catholic were recorded. Their marriage was performed at Morpeth on the Hunter River on 22nd November 1842 by the Reverend Thorley-Bolton, eight days after William received formal approval from the State Governor, requisite because William still was a 'Ticket of Leave man'.

Dad's father Thomas Thompson was the sixth child of a couple from the north of England, William Thompson (b. 1806 in Cumberland) and his wife Mary (nee Irvine b.1813 in Kingswater). They had sailed to Australia in 1840 as Free Settlers, with their son John (b. 11th April 1835), and daughters Ann, Barbara and Amelia (born respectively, at Cumrew, on 25th June 1836, 20th January 1838 and 4th December 1839). Amelia's daughter Ada Cummins recorded that her grandparents had intended to settle in South Africa, but a relative living in Durban, where their ship called, advised them that there were better prospects in Australia. Eight children were born to William and Mary after their arrival in New South Wales, Thomas, the only boy, being born on 17th December 1842 at the coal mining settlement of 4 Mile Creek, north of Newcastle.

The Hunter River district at that time was in the process of rapid growth, development being centred upon the town of Morpeth, which was at the head of navigation for ocean going ships, and the starting point for settlers heading for the newly opened Liverpool Plains, and to the North West. There was a great demand for native timber of all types and descriptions, and Thomas grew up into an occupation then referred to as 'Bushman', the title which he gave as his occupation when he and Susan Moore were married at Tarro NSW, on 12th May 1871. By the time that my Dad was born this occupation had come to be more clearly defined as 'Timbergetter,' and this always was the term Dad used in referring to his father, who reportedly was a powerfully built man well over 6 feet in height and of such physique that in his daily work he regularly used an axe for tree felling having a head of 6 pounds weight.

Dad often made mention to me of his father's skill in felling large trees just where he wanted them, and in hewing beams and girders out of the trunks with the use of squaring axes, both right hand and left hand models. It appears that the main source of bread and butter income came from cutting pit props for the coal mine in Minmi, operated by Mr. John Brown, who had started in coal mining at 4 Mile Creek some years earlier. Minmi at that time was a thriving community of about seven thousand people, and Mr. Brown lived there in a large house.

As an experienced timber-getting contractor Thomas was successful in his tender for supply of several hundred hewn hardwood transoms (extra depth high quality sleepers) for the new railway bridge being constructed in 1888-89 by the American Bridge Company over the Hawkesbury River to connect Newcastle with Sydney. The laying of the railway track on a newly completed road was, in those days, the exclusive function of the NSW Railways, hence Thomas' contract was not with the bridge construction contracts. This bridge was opened to rail traffic in May 1889, hence Thomas' contract would need to have been completed by January of that year to avoid delay to tracklaying. Payment by the Americans probably was prompt, and no doubt was celebrated in Thomas and Susan's household.

Dad used to relate to me how, when only a boy, he often was taken by his father into the forest to accompany him on a whole days work. As a result Dad developed a good working knowledge of the trees in the district, and the uses to which they could be put. In addition Dad soon had a reliable sense of direction in the bush (which he never lost), and learned to recognize the wildlife, especially the birds' sounds, and the appearance of their 'owners.' In later life (when I knew him) he was so good at imitating the calls of at least 8 birds, that in the bush, real birds would come down to investigate. Dad's personal whistle to Mum when walking up the side passage at home on his return from School, and indeed at any other appropriate occasion, was the call of the Grey Thrush, which Mum would answer in kind. When the Gould League of Bird Lovers was established in 1910, Dad was one of its earliest members, and took part in their bird call imitation competitions.

One aspect of his childhood which greatly affected Dad was the disastrous effect on the family of his father's addiction to alcoholic drinks, which were readily available at the hotel located adjacent to the terminus Railway Station at Minmi, and only a few hundred yards from the family home. Dad recalled to me how his father quite frequently would arrive home well after tea time, and 'much the worse for wear' (my Dad's expression), stagger into the house calling out to his wife "Any thoop Thuthan.' For the whole of his life Dad therefore was implacably opposed to what he referred to as 'the booze', and never touched it, either as he grew up or in later life. He deeply resented a trick played upon him while at Teachers' College, when his 'friends' put gin in his glass of orange juice.

The early death of Thomas Thompson at the age of 55 years in 1897, when Dad was only 8 years of age, left Susan and her family in a precarious financial position, with five children under the age of 10 years still to be raised. By this time the older members of her family had left home to be married:

Jane THOMPSON ('Jinny')	b.	1869
William THOMPSON	b.	1872
Mary THOMPSON ('Poll')	b.	1873

hence the family at the home in Minmi was made up of:

Susan THOMPSON (Mother)	Aged 52 years
Ann THOMPSON ('Nance')	b. 7.09.1876
Susannah THOMPSON	b. 11.07.1878
Elizabeth THOMPSON	b. 1880
John Thomas THOMPSON	b. 1883

Robert THOMPSON   b. 21.10.1885
Alice Catherine THOMPSON b. 24.06.1887
Joseph Walter THOMPSON   b. 17.10.1889

Susan was fortunate in still having at home her two older daughters who both were energetic and competent, hence increasingly Dad's upbringing came under their care. The effect of his father's death on John Thomas Thompson must have been traumatic, because family recollections are that he ran away from home, took to alcoholic drink, and never married, and was looked upon as 'the black sheep of the family.' His brother Robert was able to be kept at school, but in 1900, at the age of 14 years, to help family finances, he had to leave school and take a job as pit boy in the Minmi Colliery.

On 22nd April 1903 Susannah married Brook Goodall at Minmi, which left the running of the family in Ann's hands, the more so as her mother's health was failing. A family friend, John Shearston, a married man, was helpful in Dad's upbringing with advice and provision of books (including the 11th Edition of Encyclopaedia Britannica.)

With this assistance Dad became a good scholar at Minmi Public School, and on completion of his studies there, applied for, and on 29th January 1906 was appointed to the position of Pupil Teacher on Probation, at his old School, which allowed him to continue living at home. Many years later he related to me that his oldest pupil was 19 years old, and a lot bigger. During the next year Dad satisfied the requirements of the Department of Public Instruction, and on 31st May 1907 was appointed Pupil Teacher at Wickham Public School, a suburb of Newcastle, on a salary of £40 per annum.

Dad's services at Wickham in 1907 evidently were satisfactory because on 4th November of that year, he was promoted to Teacher Class II, with the appointment backdated to 22nd January 1907. One year later on 22nd January 1908 he was promoted to Teacher Class I.

During 1908 Dad won a scholarship to Sydney Teachers College (then at East Balmain) where he attended the Sessions 1909-1910, and stayed in lodgings at 65 Merton Street, Rozelle. From his remarks to me (many years later) he enjoyed the course, and although he found it strenuous, found time to act as Secretary to the College Sports Union. His best subject was English, especially English Literature, and he learned a great deal about the origins of words, notably those from Latin, which he also studied. The different shades of meaning available in the English language became important to him.

Towards the end of the course Dad, together with the rest of his class, was required to write an appreciation of a poem which he happened to like greatly and he 'opened his heart' on paper. To his consternation he was the member of the class selected by the Lecturer to stand up and read out his own work. To add to his unhappy state of mind, the rest of the class, as he finished reading, sang derisively:

"Sawdust, sawdust, it all sounds like sawdust to me, to me."

Dad told me (years later) that he decided there and then to switch from teaching English to teaching Mathematics - it would be less personally embarrassing.

Much later and after Dad's death, his sister Alice holidaying with us in Parkes in 1953, told me that her brother Joe (who as with all of the family, had been brought up in the Minmi Church of England) had had what she described as a genuine spiritual experience while in his teens. Aunty Alice explained to me that Dad wanted very much to discuss this with someone who could understand, so went to his Minister. Regrettably this man made light of Dad's experience, and told him not to take it too seriously. Aunty said that her brother, having bared his soul to a person whom he expected would have some semblance of understanding, was affronted by what he saw as hypocrisy, and from then on turned his back on the Church, and everything connected with it. As I grew up I could not help noticing that Dad 'had a scunner' (Scottish = 'had a down') on **all** Churches, but **never a**bandoned Christian principles in his dealings with people. He was especially critical of any of us kids when we presumed to judge other people for doing, or not doing something right -'People who live in glass houses,' he would snap, 'should pull down the blinds.'

Following his academic success at Balmain Teachers College in 1910, Dad was appointed to the teaching staff of Five Dock Public School. He used to tell me that he was still lodging at Rozelle as before, and that often he would run all the way to the School to keep fit, and that a big section of this run was across pleasant open country with neither roads nor houses. He evidently enjoyed his time at Five Dock School, and this is clear from the reference given to him by his Principal Mr. Fred Berman, a part of which reads as follows:

'His class is next in seniority to my own, is invariably well managed and efficient. As Teacher in Charge of such special subjects as Manual Training, Science, First Aid, Cadet Work and Nature Study, he has worked with zest and has in each and every department achieved a high measure of success. As Sportsmaster in Charge of the Swimming and Football Clubs he has been equally successful not confining his activities only to the School, but taking a prominent position in the management of the Inter Schools Competition.'

Around about this time Dad's mother Susan moved out of the Minmi home into a rented cottage at 86 Cleary Street Hamilton, a suburb of Newcastle. She shared this house with her daughters Ann ('Nance') and Alice, who in addition to caring for their mother, were pursuing their own joint career of running a dressmaking business in Newcastle.

Dad's interest in British Association football, or soccer as we came to know it, enabled him to play for Balmain first division. On June 14 1911, the *Sydney Morning Herald* noted in the game Balmain v Glebe: Thompson's long, strong kicking frequently sent the Glebe forwards back unsatisfied, and was very often the means of starting his own forwards on a goal-hunting expedition. Balmain went on to win the 1911 Gardiner Cup with Dad at full back, with the *Sydney Morning*

Herald noting on 18 September: "Balmain's win over *HMS Powerful* in the Gardiner Cup completed a chain of victories that has not been surpassed in Association football in this state. The Gardiner Cup, Association Cup, Rawson Cup and the first division of the second league competition, have all been accepted by the players of the marine suburb."

The *Evening News* noted in its edition May 6 1912, that "J. Thompson, one of Balmain's full backs, is an improved man. In several engagements that he participated in last year he did not use his head to any extent. But on Saturday that particular work was feature of his play. Most likely he has taken a lesson from Fergusson." In August 1912 Dad played fullback for NSW v Queensland, with NSW winning 3 games to 1 and his Balmain team once again won the Gardiner Cup.

The Royal Australian Navy was established as a separate entity in 1911, and John Shearston was too old to enlist. Such was his enthusiasm for the new Service, however, that he was able to persuade Dad, who had a bright future in the Department of Public Instruction, to resign and to enlist in the Navy. However, football certainly had a place in Dad's life. On 6 May 1913, the *Saturday Referee and Arrow* noted that "Balmain not having been defeated so far (in the season)... Thompson was reinstated to the full back position, his performance being creditable." *The Sydney Mail* of 28 May 1913 then published a team photograph of the Balmain District Association Football Club, with Dad top left, as 'Winners of the Gardiner Challenge Cup 1912 and Present State Champions.'

A few days later, Dad joined the R.A.N. on 1st June 1913, and was initially posted for in-service training at R.A.N. Portsea (Victoria) Naval Depot, then to the Navy's Training Ship *HMAS Tingira* (pronounced 'Ting-gyra'), which was at anchor in Rose Bay, Sydney Harbour. He was then classified as Schoolmaster, with the rank of Chief Petty Officer, and posted back to HMAS *Tingira*, where he was involved in teaching Navigation and Mathematics to Naval Cadets.

(Top) Dad, Royal Australian Navy, 1913;
(Lower) The training ship, HMAS Tingira, off Berry's Bay.

This ship had been refitted as a Naval Training Vessel from a disused passenger sailing ship of the late 1860s which originally was named *Sobraon*. She was wrought iron hulled and had been built in Aberdeen, Scotland in 1866, and regularly had plied the passenger trade between London and Melbourne via the Cape of Good Hope for many years. All of these voyages were under the command of Captain Elmslie, and were without accident of any kind, or loss of life.

In 1914, Dad was still enjoying his football. In May 1914, *The Sydney Sun* mentioned: "The first eleven of Balmain will, as usual, be a strong combination, notwithstanding that two good backs in Thompson and Rattray will be unavailable. The first named will assist the Navy." In June 1914 Dad played for NSW in both games against Victoria, in a poor NSW display (2 goals to 11), but in July *The Referee* noted Dad as one of six playing "dandy games" in that year's State Championships. He probably felt a lot better when the *SMH* noted on 22nd July 1914 details of his next Interstate game NSW v Tasmania, where NSW won with a record 11 goals to one. Dad played full back throughout that match. "Thompson and Dennis, with foot and head, repelled a rush by Tasmania..."

War broke out between Germany and Great Britain on 4th August 1914, and Australia quickly became involved because of interlock-ing Treaties, with heavy pressure being placed in its fledgling Navy, not only in patrol duties in the Pacific Ocean, but also in providing trained men for the extra fighting ships which the Federal Government acquired. Several times Dad applied for transfer to a fighting ship on active service, but each time was refused, on the grounds of an acute shortage of Instructors with his expertise. He was bluntly informed that while this shortage existed in the Navy, he would be required to serve on *Tingira*, which being at anchor in Australia, was not an Active Service posting.

In the face of the determined refusal on the part of the Navy, Dad decided to make the best of the situation by improving himself scholastically, and enrolled in the Evening (part-time) Course in Arts at the University of Sydney, for the 1917 Academic Year. Meanwhile Dad involved himself in sporting activities, and in addition found time to assist in the newly formed Public Schools Amateur Athletic Association, with contacts from his days at Five Dock Public School.

This brought him in contact with Mr. Arthur Roberts, then Principal of Smith Street Public School and a keen sportsman, and was invited to meet with him at his home 'Glenroy', 7 Tilba Avenue Balmain, from time to time to discuss P.S.A.A.A. matters. Here Dad met the family members, Marjorie, Muriel, Arthur (who always was known as 'Bob') and Alan. Marjorie was an accomplished pianist who had in 1916 been granted the Licentiate (Pianist) of the Associated Board of the Royal Academy of Music and the Royal College of Music (both in London). Also some time in 1916 Marjorie had lost, killed in action on the Somme (France) battlefield, a close friend from her Albury days, Mr. William F. White, son of a grazing family near Howlong, west of Albury.

Dad continued his football career. In May 1918, *The Referee* noted that in the Rawson Cup fixtures: For the Royal Navy Thompson and Haskins are the only connecting links between the teams of 1917 and 1918."

Dad and Marjorie became friends - her brother 'Bob' told me 80 years later that it was 'obvious that there were more reasons that P.S.A.A.A. matters for Joe's frequent visits to 'Glenroy'. Football still played a part in his life, as he assumed the captaincy of the Navy team, with *The Arrow* noting in September 1919 : "Balmain Fernleigh, who drew a bye in the initial round, join issue with Navy. The former's splendid showing in the League final should create doubts and fears in the minds of the Naval men. Thompson and Co., however, promise to give the top-notchers a hard run for it, and in order to secure the strongest team played a Possibles v. Probables match on Wednesday last. Endeavors are being made to induce Haskins to their strip. Before war service called him overseas Tiny and Joe Thompson formed the full-back line of the team."

Soon after Dad and Marjorie Roberts married. The ceremony took place on 15th December 1919, but not in a Church, although a Presbyte-rian Minister officiated, but in the sitting room of 'Glenroy', which was unusual at that time. If there were photographs taken, they have been lost. The couple spent the early part of their marriage in a cottage on the eastern side of Balfour Road Rose Bay, at the corner with Latimer Road, within sight of *Tingira* at anchor. Dad had completed all the requirements of the University Arts Course before the wedding, and on 24th April 1920 he graduated Bachelor of Arts - coincidentally this was his new mother-in-law's 53rd birthday. The war had ended in Novem-ber 1918, but the Navy still was active, and on 27th April 1920 Dad was transferred to *HMAS Encounter* which took voyages to Port Philip Bay (Vic.), and to Albany (WA). The magnificent harbour and the surround-ing country at Albany impressed Dad greatly. He recounted to me later that it was from this port on Christmas Day 1918, (before he joined) that *Encounter* had been ordered to proceed at maximum speed to Darwin, Northern Territory, to rescue the Administrator, Dr. Gilruth, from civil insurrection. A Company of Marines from on board *Encounter* did the job on arrival in Darwin Harbour, and evacuated Dr. Gilruth to the ship, which then returned to Perth WA at normal cruising speed.

On 1st October 1920, Dad was transferred to *HMAS Sydney*, a bat-tleship then based in Sydney Harbour. Marjorie and other wives of the Ships Company were invited to accompany their spouses on a short final voyage outside Sydney Heads prior to decommissioning (and later scuttling) of this fine ship. During this voyage, the ship's main arma-ment - 6 inch guns - were fired, a terrifying experience Mum related to me years afterwards, and understandably, as she was by then 7 months pregnant with me.

On 23rd December 1920 I was born in the back bedroom (on the top floor) at 'Glenroy' - her Christmas present to Dad. Mum told me years later that her shrieks could be heard in Glassop Street. I was given the names Geoffrey Arthur, the first after Dad's nephew, Geoff Wheeler, and the second after Mum's father. I could truthfully say that 'I am a son of the Navy'.

Balmain District Association Football Club.
WINNERS OF THE GARDINER CHALLENGE CUP, 1912, AND PRESENT STATE CHAMPIONS
Back Row (Heading Left to Right). — J. Thompson, R. B. Hughes, B. Ferguson. Second Row. — J. Richards, R. T. Black, I. Black, — ? , A. Latta. Third Row. — J. Ferguson,J. McDonald,sen.,R. H. Moore(Capt.), C. Thorpe, N. Charlton. On Ground.— J. McDonald, jun.,W. Robertson, A. O'Hehir.

MUDGEE

On 26th January 1921 Dad was discharged from the R.A.N., and his application for re-engagement with the Education Department in NSW was approved, and his posting was to Mudgee High School as Teacher of Mathematics. My parents and I moved to Mudgee quite soon from the temporary home at 'Glenroy,' and lived in a rented cottage on Norman Street, looking down on the town. Before long, a friendly light brown coloured dog of nondescript antecedents adopted our family, to become a devoted member of the household - the name was 'Tinker.'

My brother was born in Mudgee on 29th July 1922, and given the names 'David Shearston' - the first being after an Uncle of Mum's, the second after John Shearston. Not long afterwards, Dad moved the family closer to town into larger premises which were the lower floor of a substantial brick two storey house on the north side of Court Street, just east of the railway line to Gulgong. The house (now numbered 76) also had a name which assumed almost mystical proportions with Mum in later years - 'Kildallen.'

My earliest recollections are of the crisp atmosphere, and of the hot dry days of summer during which Dave and I used to play in the aromatic shade of the big pepper trees lining the driveway to the house,

Marjorie and Joe Thompson, with Geoff, at their first home in Mudgee 1921. Photograph by Esme Hadley.

with toy wooden railway engines made by Dad, the nearby busy railway to Gulgong added reality to our games. But there was danger also in the stubble paddock separating our house from the railway, it was easy to run a piece of straw into an eye, and there were lengths of rusty barbed wire scattered through the stubble - we kept out. Another danger was in the fowlyard at the rear of 'Kildallen' where Dad kept some chooks; it was impressed upon me that to cut one's foot in that yard could bring on 'lockjaw' (the old name for tetanus) which had caused the death of my cousin Ronald Wheeler who had run a thorn into his foot while playing in a horse paddock alongside the home of Dad's eldest sister 'Jinny" in Hamilton, only in 1919.

A friendship developed between our parents and a teacher of German at the High School, Miss Esme Hadley, and she continued to visit us after we moved into 'Kildallen.' Esme was an enthusiastic amateur photographer, and took most of the photographs of our family for some years. Other friends were the Shortland family, the father Percy, also being a High School teacher colleague of Dad's. Percy was studying privately to fit himself to enter the NSW Justice Department, where subsequently he rose to be a Judge. His son John and I were good friends.

Feeling the need for some means of getting out into the country, Dad purchased from Lonergans Store in Mudgee in March 1924, a new Overland Model 91 touring car. This had a 4 cylinder petrol engine, a canvas hood and the body was a sandy olive green colour. Years later Dad explained to me that the alternative was a Model T Ford, but the Overland had a 3 speed gearbox (only 2 speed in the Ford) and better body lines, as well as offering a choice of colour - only black was the Ford offering. The registered number of Overland was 65-103.

Like most light cars of that era, Overland's wheels had 12 wooden spokes made out of American hickory, and the pneumatic tyres were of 3½ inch section requiring 60 pounds per square inch of air pressure. Brakes were fitted to the rear wheels only, and there were no shock absorbers, hence the ride was 'firm.' Petrol came in 4 gallon tinplate containers packed in pairs in a strong wooden box. Neither bowsers nor service stations existed in Mudgee up to the time we left.

Nevertheless Dad took us all, sometimes with Esme as a passenger, on numerous local trips in this car, including a memorable one (to me at least) to the Cement Works at Kandos, on the road to Lithgow - the overhead cableway system which went for miles across country carrying raw materials to the Works left a lasting impression on me.

Our stay in Mudgee was very happy, the dry climate also suited Mum who had been born in Inverell NSW, and had spent her early years in Albury. She became involved in local musical activities, and was the Musical Director of, and played for a production of the musical comedy 'San Toy' in 1924.

Dad's previous service as a teacher with the NSW Department of Public Instruction was not recognized by the Department because of a curious internal Regulation which required a teacher to have enlisted in the Armed Forces **after** the outbreak of war in 1914 and/or had seen Active Service during the war. Dad had enlisted in 1913 and through no fault of his own, had not seen Active Service. By this rule Dad was required to fit himself for promotion by sitting for a 'Regulation Ib Examination' from which teachers who had remained in the service of the Department of Public Instruction during the war and **never** enlisted were exempted! Dad refused as a matter of principle to sit for this examination (which he would had had no difficulty passing), hence was debarred permanently from promotion, whilst the stay-at-home teachers, most of whom were junior to him, were promoted, many to the rank of Principal. I distinctly remember several acrimonious arguments between our parents on this matter.

Whether or not this attitude came into the consideration, Dad was transferred at the end of 1924 to North Sydney Boys High School. All of our furniture and heavy luggage was removed from 'Kildallen' to Mudgee Railway Station, thence by train to Sydney (which resulted in

(Top) Dad with the 1924 Overland, Mudgee, with Geoff and Mum in the back seat; (lower) Mudgee 1924, with Geoff in his perambulator. Photos by Esme Hadley.

less damage than by road in those days). We then set out on the journey to Sydney in the Overland with Mum (7 months pregnant) and Dave in the front with Dad, and me, nearing 4 years old, in the back seat.

At about Lithgow steady rain set in and extra care was needed on the wet gravel road. Everything was going well until on the steep western descent to the Lett River, Dad was using the brakes only (not in gear) when the rear wheels lost grip ('skittered' was Dad's expression) on the corrugated gravel pavement on a sharp left hand bend swinging the rear of the car around suddenly and smashing the O.S. rear wheel. This was fortuitous because the drag quickly stopped the car, with the front almost touching some large white painted rocks, placed by the (then) Main Roads Board to mark the edge, above a 200 foot steep drop. Drizzling rain continued as we all got out and found that no one was injured, and the car intact except for the wrecked wheel. Before long a man driving a large 1924 Sunbeam tourer towards Sydney stopped to help, and Mum and us boys were given a fast trip right through to Balmain (he said that it was not much out of his way) and refused to accept any money. The rain continued for this trip and the driver had his hood **down**, but travelled so fast that we hardly got wet at all. Dad got a lift back into Lithgow to seek help and for overnight stay. Overland was picked up by mechanics next day and tted with a new rear wheel. The only loss was a neat nickel plated clearance lamp on the O.S. front mudguard which Dad had fitted as an extra. This had been thieved by a passerby, but its absence did not deter Dad from driving through to 'Glenroy,' which was to become our temporary home. After this episode Dad invariably descended steep hills in second gear.

'Glenroy' was an impressive two storey brick house with a slate roof, set on a steep hillside facing west, and had a water frontage to Iron Cove, which joins Parramatta River. The Roberts had moved into this house, then only a few years old, in 1906 after Grandpa's transfer from Albury Superior Public School in June 1904. There were four bedrooms on the top floor with a bathroom, and a marvellous balcony looking out over the water. On the ground floor there was another balcony backed up by a large sitting room, then through big folding doors to another large room containing bookcases and a three quarter sized billiard table. Further back and half into the hillside were the breakfast room and the combined kitchen/laundry. The only toilet was outside. Our parents moved into the spare bedroom (in which I had been born) with Dave and me. The Overland was parked in Tilba Avenue.

Before long Mum brought home a baby sister for us boys, born on 1st March 1925 at North Sydney Hospital. Apparently there had been long discussions over the name to be given to the little girl, and finally it had been agreed that 'Nance Elizabeth' would be appropriate - Nance after the nickname of Dad's elder sister Ann, and Elizabeth after Grandma Roberts and Dad's sister Elizabeth wife of William Wheeler who ran a butchers shop on the south side of Darling Street East Balmain, at the top of the hill above the wharf. Unfortunately Dad was overcome by the excitement on his way to the Registry, and, unable to remember the exact **final** decision, registered our new sister as 'Elizabeth Nance."

Outside 'Glenroy', Balmain, Winter 1935. Back Row: Mum, John Roberts, Grandpa Arthur Roberts, Dad, Bill Cameron, Muriel Cameron, Grandma Bess Roberts; Seated: Dave, Joe, (behind Mary), Lin Cameron, Geoff, Bob Cameron, Marj Roberts and Doug Cameron. Photo Alan Roberts.

WILLOUGHBY

The accommodation at 'Glenroy' was decidedly cramped so Dad, with the help of a £950 loan from Grandpa Roberts, purchased a newly completed 2 bedroom brick, and tile roofed cottage at No. 102 Lyle Street East Willoughby, from 'spec' builders, Green Brothers. The house was well finished with open front verandah to the east, 3 tiled fireplaces (one of which was a dummy), gas stove in the kitchen and a bathroom containing a cast iron porcelain enamel bath (white) on legs, with a gas heater for water (no shower for hot water at that early stage.) The back verandah also was open, and exposed to the westerly winds; the laundry was outside, and alongside it was a sewered toilet. Most of the houses in Lyle Street shared this internal layout but were rescued from anonymity by changes in the roof design. Lyle Street then was an unformed earth track ending in cliffs about ¼ mile north and south of McClelland Street, which gave access to Forsyth Street and the tramline, a walk of ¾ mile past Willoughby Park and corner shops at Second Avenue and High Street. When we first went there a good bus service was provided to Lyle Street by the White Transit Bus Coy, but was expensive, so Dad drove himself to School most times or walked to the tram.

We were very happy to be in our new home. At weekends and after School Dad set about making a vegetable garden at the rear of the block. Dad also used to take Dave and me for walks into the bush which lined the whole of the opposite (east) side of Lyle Street, and we were introduced to the various native trees and flowers which grew there plentifully.

As Overland was an open tourer Dad felt that providing some shelter was quite urgent, and soon set about building a fibro sheeted timber framed garage with a corrugated iron roof and timber double doors. He located this west of the house and of sufficient extra length to fit in his carpenter's bench and large toolbox. Being the 'big boy' I was pressed into service as a labourer, firstly to help break up bush rocks with an engineer's hammer, down to no more than 1 inch in size. When there was enough Dad would mix the stones with creek sand and cement, using a square mouthed shovel, and my job then was to add water to the dry materials as Dad turned them over, until a satisfactory looking grey 'porridge' resulted. Dad then shovelled the mix into forms marking out the floor slabs, finally smoothing over with a steel tool which he called a 'float'.

After the garage came the footpaths and Dad dragged flagstones up from the bush in a solid 'billy cart' which he made with a pair of 8 inch diameter cast iron wheels. To make the paths I was his helper whilst he cut the stones into interlocking shapes using a steel chisel 4 inches wide, which he called a 'bolster'. The cut flagstones then were set in sand (also from the bush) leaving gaps about 1 inch wide between each stone. A cement/sand/water mixture then was sliced into the open joints and smoothed over with a steel trowel. We were the first in Lyle Street to have such interesting looking paths. Mr. Thias next door in No. 100 showed his admiration by doing his paths the same way.

I started school in Kindergarten at Willoughby Public School, a walk of about 1½ miles, in January 1926. My teacher, Miss Armstrong, had a most precise way of speaking, 'pencil' was pronounced 'pen sill', which quite entranced me, and I was repeating this to myself, inaudibly I thought. Miss A. however did hear, considered me cheeky, and chastised me physically - not an auspicious start for the first week of my formal education.

On Dad's 37th birthday 17th October 1926, our young brother Joe was born, also at the North Sydney Hospital, and his arrival in the house created a need for more space. So Dad, always a man of action, widened the back verandah by about 4 feet, walled in the northern end with fibro sheeting, erected fibro sheeted walls on the western side, which had window openings 4 feet high the full length, enclosed with galvanised fly wire, and protected from the westerly weather by 2 large roll-up canvas blinds fitted outside. Access to the laundry and toilet was given by relocating the kitchen door to the new south western corner of the now quite snug verandah. Dave and I moved into the new space and were very comfortable, even though the blinds banged a lot in the westerly gales; we were not at all bothered by the 6 inch square timber post left in the middle of our room, which supported the main roof of the house.

Dad was a man of many parts; in addition to these jobs he maintained the car himself (except for big jobs), repaired all our shoes properly by hand sewing on a replacement leather sole, and made his vegetable garden very productive. In between times he continued with his hobby of cabinet work in Australian native timbers; Queensland Maple and Red Cedar were his favourites.

For this especial of his interests Dad had no power tools, just good saws, chisels and smoothing planes. He kept all tools sharp and never used a pencil for marking out - always a scriber which was a chisel shaped tool in which the sharp edge was set at an angle of about 60 degrees to the axis of the tool. When his joints were finished it was difficult to detect them, especially after he had French polished the timber, which he also did himself, by hand.

Dad's vegetable garden was neatly laid out with thin bush flat stones marking the edges of the beds which were accessed by walkways about 18 inches wide. I was introduced to weeding at an early age, but the product almost made it worthwhile with the possible exceptions of broad beans and swede turnips. Somehow they never did match my palate, nor do they now, although I have since found that turnips grown in a frosty area lose their acrid taste. Dad's garden often had need of seedlings, so he would despatch me to the nearest Nurseryman, a Mr. Bannatyne, who ran his business on a landlocked acre of beautiful rich loam soil on the banks of a little creek on the eastern side of Ann Street. Mr. B. was well into his 60s, but active and his stock was good quality.

The combined effect of Dad's lean and practical upbringing, and teacher experience made him concise in his thinking and often he would require of us that we 'look for the 'nub'' of a problem, that is the factor or condition about which the problem depended. His Navy experience built terseness into his speech, and whilst he never used bad language (which he regarded as a sign of an empty mind) his speech had a sprinkling of colourful seafaring jargon, of which the following are some examples:

Bow	= Front of anything moveable, car, pram etc.
Stern	= Rear " " " " " "
Port	= Left side of " " " " "
Starboard	= Right side of " " " " "
Adrift	= Anything which had become detached, unstuck.
Stove-in	= Anything so damaged as to have lost its shape.
Lee-side	= Side of anything, house, tent, etc. away from wind.
Shipshape	= Everything tidy and in order, ready for use.
Loaded to the Plimsoll	= Anything moveable loaded to maximum safe capacity.

Getting one's sea legs =	Becoming used to any kind of new situation.
Gangway =	Any part of house or yard used frequently (We kids often were in trouble for 'blocking the gangway' by casually leaving toys etc. just where someone would fall over them, eg. in the dark)
All hands on deck =	All children required to help him.
All hands and the cook=	" " " " " " plus Mum.
Weigh enough, toss and boat your oars; often shortened to: Weigh enough. =	Stop whatever you are doing for him (reference to order needed to be given by Officer in Charge of Naval pinnace to oarsmen as boat nears wharf/ship. Weigh enough means stop rowing. Toss your oars meant hold oars vertically to avoid damage/personal injury; boat your oars meant to lay oars longitudinally in boat.
Sighted off Nobbys =	On occasion when someone in a crowd, or something (screw, etc.) lost inexplicably, has been sighted/found. (Reference to daily reports in Newcastle press of ships sighted off Nobbys Lighthouse at mouth of the Hunter River).

Dad had a short temper and expected us, especially us boys, to 'spring to it' (another Navy expression) upon receiving his instructions, failing which appropriate chastisement would be administered, often swiftly and on the spot. Being the eldest, I received the brunt of these.

In addition to his Navy parlance, Dad regularly made use of the following colloquialisms:

Barmy	= Foolish, silly.
Beano	= Feast, extravagant party.
Blatherskite	= Voluble self-promoting person.
Bloke	= Male person (neutral/anonymous).
Bob	= Shilling.
Bonzer	= Excellent.
Bundle, drop one's	= Give up hope
Bushed	= Lost, confused.
Chest, get it off one's	= Express one's feelings.
Clobber	= Raiment, vesture.
Cocky's Joy	= Golden syrup.
Codger	= An old bloke.
Coot	= Bloke who is known/regarded adversely.
Cove	= Bloke who is known/regarded favourably.
Dizzy limit	= Outrageous; usually applied to behaviour.
Fiver	= Five pound note.
Galoot	= Simpleton.
Guff	= Nonsense talk about a serious matter.
Gutser, come a	= Fall headlong.
Guyver	= Make-believe/gushing talk.
Guzzle	= Consume excessively, regardless of consequences.
High falutin'	= Boastfully pompous.
John Hop	= Policeman.
King Pin	= Any person of chief importance.
Lid	= Hat.
Lid, Dip the	= Raise one's hat (male only).
Moniker	= One's name, title or signature.
Nark	= Spoil sport.
Nick	= Physical condition.
Nipper	= Any small child - and five of us nippers.
Peeled, keep one's eyes	= Keep a sharp lookout.

Phizog/Phiz	=	The face.
Pip, the	=	Fit of depression/frustration.
Quid	=	One pound note.
Sandy blight	=	Conjunctivitis.
Savvy	=	Common sense.
Scalded cat, run like a	=	Travel exceedingly fast.
Shickered	=	Intoxicated (alcoholic).
Skerrick, not a	=	No trace at all.
Skite	=	To boast (verb), boastful person (noun).
Spank	=	To chastise (usually on buttocks).
Spout	=	To speak at length.
Spuds	=	Potatoes.
Squiz	=	A brief glance.
Stoush	=	Serious fighting.
Stumped	=	Unable to continue (as in cricket).
Swanky	=	Ostentatious (usually expensively).
Swig	=	Draught of any liquid.
Tenner	=	Ten pound note.
Toff	=	Exalted person.
Togs	=	Garments for swimming, work, official duties.
Trey bit	=	Threepenny piece (silver).
Underconstumble	=	Comprehend with effort.
Wallop	=	Beat, chastise (I was often walloped).
Yap	=	To talk volubly and interminably/irrelevantly.

Dad always expressed himself clearly and succinctly, nevertheless he laid claim to what he called 'the Irishman's Right,' as his Grandmother came from Tipperary in Ireland, and he explained this to me as follows:

"An Englishman knows the King's English, and is allowed to speak once only; A Scotsman has difficulty with the King's English, so is allowed to speak twice; An Irishman has difficulties with all languages, hence is allowed to speak until he is understood."

Dad had an original way of looking at things, and this affected me personally early in life, as I had been born left handed. In the 1920s this was regarded as something of a calamity, and most parents endeavoured to correct the 'fault' by beatings. However in 1926 when I first went to School, Dad decided on a new 'tack' (another Navy expression), he knew how keenly interested I was in MECCANO sets, the construction toy of those days, so promised me one of these just as soon as I could prove to him that I could write with my **right** hand. This was a most powerful incentive to me, and to his surprise at the end of only three weeks I was writing quite creditably with the 'correct' hand - he was pleased (and relieved) to honour his promise, with Set No. 1, and in retrospect, started me on a career in engineering.

In 1928 big changes took place in my life as I moved up into the 'Big School'. To start with the handsome new white school buildings faced Oakville Road which shortened the walk from home. Then I found that the boys were separated from the girls, at opposite ends of the building. I was in Class 3A and my Teacher was Mr. Kohlhoff, a stocky man of Russian origin, with a thick accent - we boys were a bit scared of him, although he never chastised any of us. In those days the Boys Section of the School was at the eastern end of the building, and the Girls Section was at the end nearest the Post Office. Class 3A did not have a proper classroom but was conducted in part of the long hall which ran for most of the length of building facing Oakville Road.

Most of the playground was dirt and very suitable for playing Marbles, and I soon learned the difference between clay dabs (which broke fairly easily) and glass marbles, some of which were regarded highly because of the internal pattern visible through the translucent outer glass envelope. At the top of the scale were those made from natural agate, referred to with awe as 'Connie Agates' - very expensive. However, to be feared was any boy who had managed to acquire a 'Steelie'. These could not be bought anywhere, they only could come out of a discarded ball race, which limited the sources. A half inch 'Steelie' in the hands of a good player could smash just about any opponents marble.

The other game which occupied a lot of our attention was Peg Tops. These came in various sizes but usually were 1 ½ inches in diameter at the top and tapering down to a point which was tipped with a special steel pin. A piece of flexible string was wound around the tapered section starting at the pin, then holding the loose end of the string throw the top down smartly to the ground causing it to unwind and spin the top. The smartest trick in this game was to land your top straight above your opponent's - not easily done!

In wet weather we would retreat to the 'Weather Shed', a weatherboard structure about 35 feet square and open to the east. Unfortunately the timber floor was not suitable for marbles.

At the southern end of the playground was a wonderfully interesting looking piece of vacant wilderness land owned by the Education Department, complete with well grown trees suitable for climbing. Regrettably we were banned from even setting foot in it - snakes were given as the reason.

'Big School' opened new horizons for me - shops started to be interesting places. First there was the single fronted shop on the north side of Oakville Road known as 'Mum and Dads', which had a window display of essential items such as pencils, rubbers, set squares and rulers, but inside the shop, which you did not dare enter without money, was a glass fronted display of mouth watering cakes - my ambition became to have a large cream bun. However my parents invariably provided me with a very adequate cut lunch and only enough coins for essentials, so cream buns remained out of reach for the time being.

There was another shop in Oakville Road on the south eastern corner of Keary Street, which seemed mainly to serve the surrounding houses. However they did something different for us kids - in the window facing the School there was always a marvellous display, changed every few weeks, of fireworks - 'crackers' was our term. They had everything from No.1 firecrackers ('Tom Thumbs'), No.2's which were louder, small and large bungers, double bungers (which exploded twice) to split cane covered 'basket bombs' (which could be outright dangerous). Of course there were the elegant (and expensive) devices such as Roman Candles, Catherine Wheels, Flower Pots and Sky Rockets. We all saved our pennies to buy something for 'Cracker Night', which occurred on 24th May each year - the official name was Empire Day.

The next year 1929, I moved up to Class 4A which was in a proper classroom opening to the long hall I had been in last year. Our Teacher was Mr. Lawson, a tall wiry man with dark hair, who every morning used to enter the School grounds via Eaton Street (which then extended west of Keary Street), pause for a moment at the gate for a good look around the playground, then put his head down and make a beeline for the nearest corner of the School building, trailing a slightly battered Gladstone Bag. We thought he was the son of Australian writer Henry Lawson, and he had a nickname for most of the boys in his class, and once given, was never departed from in addressing that boy. My Mother had received from her bowls playing Dad (my Grandpa Roberts) a white jumper which he no longer fitted, but which suited me fine that winter. The very first day I wore it, Mr. Lawson pointed me out as the 'Polar Bear', and invariably addressed me thus. My mate Eyre, was short and had a wizened up sort of face - he was called the

'Mugwump'. As this had been his practice in former years, the traditional name for Mr. Lawson was 'Soapy Sam'.

As might (in retrospect) be expected, our Teacher was very keen on passing on to us the importance of words in the English language and their meanings, and of course their correct spelling. I found this very interesting, and became quite good at spelling, often leaving the others behind - having what I now recognize as a 'photographic memory' helped a lot. The other matter which Mr. Lawson insisted we learn was how to tell the time from the big wall clock outside the classroom above the Headmaster's Office. Any one of us could be instructed to go out and tell him the time - and it had better be right, for he always checked.

One day Mr. Lawson was absent sick, and our class was taken by the Headmaster, Mr. Elston, a stocky man who was a friend of Grandpa Roberts, who was Headmaster of a school in another suburb. Mr. Elston also played bowls, and seeing my white jumper (the only one in the Class) stood me up and quizzed me on the rules of that game. Very embarrassing - Grandpa Roberts had not got around to telling me, I did not even know what the 'jack' was.

In 1930 I went into Class 5A, and my Teacher was Mrs Carroll, who was a widowed lady with teenage sons, and it so happened lived not far from us in McClelland Street on the corner of Tyneside Avenue. She was a capable teacher who tolerated no cheekiness, any boy who stepped out of line was sent around to Mr. Elston's Office to receive cuts of the cane. She was keen on Mathematics and I learned to work tidily to avoid errors, and was quite proud of myself when I had mastered the art of working out the square root of any given number. When I told Grandma Roberts, who had been a Teacher in her young days, she was pleased, but said: 'Now you are ready to learn how to work out the Cube Root'.

I was somewhat dashed by this new challenge, but alas, this particular item had since been removed from the official curriculum, I never did find out. Nevertheless after the peculiar, but far from dull, atmosphere last year, I appreciated being regarded as 'Geoff Thompson', a human being with a possible future.

The following year I moved up to Class 6A, which was conducted in the room located at the extreme north eastern corner of the School Building. Our Teacher was Mr. Fred Brook, a very experienced and capable teacher who hailed from the Monaro District, and often would tell us about the great high plains around Cooma; the name of course was pronounced 'Mon air oh'. He explained Australia's system· of self-government, how the Commonwealth Government came into being, and the importance of the Constitution. Then he would give us informative talks on Hygiene and Morals. I was really enjoying learning. However I had little self-confidence and was too terrified to stand up before the class to deliver a 2 minute lecturette on Captain Cook (although I well knew the subject); 2 cuts of the cane for that!

My friends in 6A were two Jacks. First was Jack Hough, who was top of the Class, and whose real names, curiously, were 'Mervyn William'. Then there was Jack McHarg, who was younger than I, and although a good student, was compelled by his parents to repeat 6th Class. Many years later Jack Hough became State M.P. for Wollongong, and was most pleased to see me. The other Jack however went on to become a Bank Manager, and treated me with cool disdain, 30 years down the track.

Dad's capacity for original thinking was a help when the Government introduced laws prohibiting people owning a couple of cows from selling milk, as Mr. Page had been to us, unless the cows were tested, etc. Dad got over this hurdle by buying a half share in a cow from Mr. Page, who lived in Lyle Street north of McClelland Street, and owned **three** cows. We nippers had the daily job of collecting milk in a clean billycan, and each morning paying Mr. Page for feeding Dad's half share of the cow from which the milk came. Exactly which cow was the subject of this deal never was explained to me, but the Depression was well on, and the arrangement was mutually satisfactory.

An Italian family named Lubrano lived in McClelland Street opposite Ann Street, and Dad had got to know him on the days they both took the tram. They had a family of four children, and when the fifth arrived, Mr. Lubrano often was delayed in the mornings helping his wife to get the other children ready for School. If this happened to coincide with the day that Dad drove himself in Overland, he would give Mr. Lubrano a lift to Crows Nest where he ran a tailoring business, and would tell Dad that he did not mind spending extra time with his children 'because he loved them'. Dad let me (only) know that he disapproved of such overt signs of affection.

A curious happening at Balmoral Beach attracted his ire. The Theosophists, a Christian sect started by an American Mrs Annie Besant, had become convinced from the writings of the Hebrew prophet Daniel, that the Second Coming of Messiah (Christ) would occur in 1935. They also were convinced (no explanations were available) that He would be in the form of one Krishnamurti, an Indian mystic protege of Mrs Besant, and furthermore that His arrival would be at Sydney Harbour opposite Balmoral Beach. It was here on a commanding site that the Theosophists at considerable expense had erected a fine Grecian style amphitheatre, open to the sky, in which enthusiasts had subscribed up to one hundred pounds to reserve a seat complete with individual brass nameplates. A Radio Station 2GB had been set up in 1926 to broadcast details of the expected great event, its call sign being named after a Theosophist 'patron saint' one Giordano Bruno. Dad's distaste for these theological imaginings was profound.

Dad was naturally artistic, although he was not 'arty'; a painting needed to have a reasonable resemblance to the real thing to arouse his interest. In his woodwork he often would slip in a curve where most artisans would have used a straight line, and even though this involved him in extra work; examples could be found in the curves he introduced in the valances of his bookcases instead of the more usual straight line, and the 'serif' curved ends he always put on the top cross pieces of his pergolas - a lot more work but quite stylish. He was interested in music, but only when he could discern a melody line - his favourite piece was Schumann's 'Devotion', which Mum often would play for him during her post-washup evening piano practice. Before the days of radio this always went for at least an hour, during which Dad was very content to sit in a comfortable chair marking Maths test papers from his School classes listening to her. He was quietly very proud of her abilities, which we kids took for granted, but which in retrospect, were very considerable. (Associateships from London College of Music, and from Trinity College London respectively at ages 14 years and 18 years; and Licentiate of the Associated Board of the Royal Academy of Music and of the Royal College of Music in 1916, at the age of 23 years). Dad confided to me once that he was baffled by large and elaborate works, such as symphonies, in which melodies were transposed and inverted, something which to Mum was as interesting as 'an open book'.

Mum's younger brother Alan had become very interested in the new technology of 'wireless' and shortly after we moved into 102 Lyle Street made a crystal receiver set for us. This required a large outdoor aerial (antenna) and Dad put up a pair of 20 foot poles on the south side of the house, about 40 feet apart. The set itself sat on the mantel-piece in the dining room above the fireplace (which we regularly used in winter). The heart of this receiver was an 8mm cube of galena held in a metal cup with small screws, and the listener had to find on its surface a sensitive spot which would rectify the incoming signal, using a piece of fine springy wire attached to a moveable arm, so that sound would result in the headphones. This little piece of wire was known as the 'catswhisker' and a small jolt could interrupt the programme. It was possible to share by unhooking one of the headphones from the headset and handing it to someone else, who had to be no further away than about three feet. Occasionally when called away in the middle of a programme, the listener would forget the connecting wire and the whole set would be brought crashing to the floor; Dad had to bolt it to the mantelpiece eventually.

Uncle Alan who was an Officer in the Commonwealth Bank at Forbes, noticed all this on one of his holiday visits, and in the early 1930s built a mains powered 4 valve receiver (3 valves and rectifier), which brought in all Sydney radio broadcasting stations plus several interstate stations after dark, via a loudspeaker, we all could hear now! Dad's part in this was to make a suitable cabinet, which he did, out of maple timber, French polished as usual. Uncle Alan was very fussy about sound quality, and went to a lot of trouble to ensure that Mum's musical ear was not disappointed. We all were very pleased when Dad had finished the cabinet, and installed the set with its speaker, and would listen for hours. We kids soon came to know the serial dramas, and there was not a little friction over which would be listened to. Of course there were also broadcasts of recorded music, and now and then a full orchestral Concert came from Sydney Town Hall, which Mum would listen to. There was now so much competition that somehow Mum's regular evening 'practises' dropped away, to be replaced by once weekly trios, involving besides herself Fred Hughes, a good violinist from Laurel Street, and Mr. Nunn who was a cellist, and so keen that he would carry his instrument half a dozen blocks from Victoria Avenue, and he had one wooden leg! After about two hours of playing Mum would bring on supper, then Dad, who listened to it all, would drive Mr. Nunn home with his cello, in Overland. The new radio of course was turned off on these evenings, and we older kids did our homework to a musical background from the sitting room. A side effect of the new radio was that we were all exposed to advertising on the commercial stations; even now I can hear a male voice insistently announcing -

'**Start** the day well with Kinkara tea, and **remember** Mother's Choice flour in every home.'

Family picnic at Kurrajong Heights, 1938.
Back Row: Nance, Bill Cameron, Joe Thompson, Muriel Cameron, Bob
Cameron, Dave. Seated: Marjorie Thompson, Uncle Bob Roberts, Geoff, Mary,
Joe, Grandma and Grandpa Roberts (Bess and Arthur)

BEACHES

Dad was of average height (recorded by the Navy as 5 feet 8 and ¾ inches) and was stockily built, but was able to move very fast, and was one of the first men in NSW to learn the (then) revolutionary swimming style of 'out of water arm recovery' based on the unique Australian Aboriginal method of swimming, which became known as the 'Australian Crawl' (now in use worldwide, because of the superior speed which it makes possible), and Dad was good at it.

He held Medals for Lifesaving, and was determined that we should share his love of the water, so, in summertime on most Saturdays he would take us all in Overland to Mona Vale Beach, where he would park the car on westerly sloping ground at the southern end among gnarled old banksia trees. It was then a remote area, occasionally we shared the plentiful space with a couple of other cars. From here we would walk straight across to the beach, where Dad would scan the surf and if he decided that it was safe, (there were no patrols) we would spend some time in it. Then we would walk along the beach with its wonderful golden pink crunchy sand to the rock pool at the northern end for more sedate swimming. Afterwards we would go back along the beach to the car and have a late picnic lunch of which Mum had left the 'makings' in the car (nothing ever was stolen), then it was back home to Willoughby, sunburnt and happily tired.

Most times Dad took the sealed road through Mosman to the Spit Bridge over Middle Harbour, then to Balgowlah and Condamine Street and northerly through DeeWhy and Narrabeen to Mona Vale. I was interested in the electric trams which went for miles alongside the road just like a railway. An occasional variation was to cross the Harbour by the (then new) concrete bridge at East Roseville to Terrey Hills (all bush then) and easterly along a gravel road to make the somewhat perilous ascent of Tumble Down Dick Hill with its challenging pair of reverse hairpin bends on a very steep pinch, then down to the northern end of Mona Vale beach - no trees for shelter here at that end, so we picnicked on a rug spread on the sand.

Dad did take us to other beaches, Balmoral beach was close handy, and was good for quiet swimming (no surf) but was somewhat 'city-fied.' Avalon beach north of Mona Vale was reached only after negotiating an atrociously rough road; Cronulla we visited once only, was interesting but a long way from Willoughby.

Geoff taking family movies at the Mona Vale rockpool in 1935.

CASTLE HILL FARM

In October 1929 the Stock Market collapsed in the USA, and this soon led to a worldwide major financial depression. The effect on Australia at first was small except for people who were dependent upon overseas investments for their income, as were the Morrisons, who were living in a new home in Epping Avenue Eastwood. Dad's sister Nance had married a Scottish merchant navy engineer. Their retirement investments, particularly in Malayan Tin Mines, had become unproductive and practically worthless. They decided to come out of retirement and take up poultry farming at Castle Hill where they had purchased the western half of a 10 acre farm ('Alston Egg Farm') run by the Pretyman family on the southern side of Tuckwells Lane, and had arranged for a builder to erect on their 5 acre block a two bedroom weatherboard home with a corrugated iron roof, plus a brick incubator room for producing the 'livestock.' Finance was found by selling the Eastwood home which was something of a wrench because of its comfort, and wonderful flower and vegetable gardens which they had made by themselves from scratch.

In 1930 Dad often took us to the farm in Overland at weekends and we sometimes stayed overnight to enable him to undertake an extensive programme of construction of sheds, starting with a long weatherboard building running east-west. Dave and I were pressed into creosoting the dozens of weatherboards before they were put up. Included in this long shed was a double garage at the end next to Pretymans, then an adjoining slightly bigger room for storage of feed for the fowls, there was also a big mixing machine. There were also sheds to be built to house the fowls, and when these had been completed, a brooder house, purchased complete on site from a poultry farmer at Revesby, had to be dismantled and put on the Ford 1 ton truck owned by a neighbour in Castle Hill, Mr. Gilham who brought all the pieces to Morrison's farm in several loads. Then came the big job of re-erecting it all - Dad was kept busy - so were Dave and I.

In return Aunty Nance always gave us great meals, cooked on the Bega wood fuel stove, eggs, and sacks of Valencia oranges from a ¼ acre orchard planted years before by the Pretymans in the south western part of the block when it was theirs. Of course there were great bags of fowl manure for Dad's garden; these were carried back to Willoughby lashed to the O.S. running board of Overland.

In between work we kids enjoyed ourselves playing in the undeveloped ½ acre on the western side of the farm, where there many wattle trees growing, and on hot days we would go for a cool off/dip in one of the two dams which had been excavated by the Pretymans before the arrival of the city water supply. They each were simply a hole about 15 feet wide cut in the hard shale ground, and sloping down from ground level to a depth of about 12 feet over a distance of about 40 feet. It seemed to me that there must have been a 'soak" to keep them full, as there was no obvious catchment. The bottom was muddy as was the water, which was quite deep at the eastern ends; Dave got into difficulties one day and Dad had to dive in to save him from drowning.

Aunty Nance had no children of her own (she had married at the age of 44 years) but was marvellous company for us kids with her wonderful sense of humour; and always had a supply of her own baked rock cakes, with lemonade to help them go down, in between meals.

It was at Castle Hill that we met our cousins on Dad's side of the family. First there was Edna Sharp, daughter of Dad's eldest sister 'Jinny' (Jane) and Uncle Will who was a fitter in the NSW Railways. Then, there were the four Goodall girls, daughters of another of Dad's older sisters Aunty 'Suse' (Susannah) and Uncle Brook. Suse and Nance were very alike, plumpish and full of fun - nothing ever seemed to be too much trouble to these two. Also at Castle Hill we met Marjorie and Ken, whose father Bob was the nearest brother to Dad in age, and their mother Aunty Lilian. They lived at Concord and he was an Officer in the railways.

Uncle Sandy's car was a maroon coloured English Star, built in Wolverhampton U.K., and was **different**. To start with it was built to a narrow track of about 4 feet, it had detachable steel disc wheels and a 12 volt electrical system (compared with Overland's 6 volt arrangement) and it had a 4 speed gearbox. However like our car its radiator tended to 'boil' on steep hills; climbing Bulli Pass was a big problem for the Star.

Other cousins we started to meet were the Wheeler boys, Harold and Geoff, and to a less extent, Cecil, sons of Dad's older sister Elizabeth, who had died in tragic circumstances in 1919. Their father, Uncle Will, although having re-married, still kept in touch with Dad, and at quite frequent intervals.

Aunty Alice, who stayed with us at Willoughby 4 nights a week, came out to Castle Hill by train on Friday nights, and stayed with Morrisons the other 3 nights to help her sister - Uncle Sandy in his thick Scots accent used to refer to her (in absentia) as 'the ludger'. We kids had to get used to being asked to bring him the 'sah' (saw), or to get something from the 'lah-undry' (laundry); I often was sent on a walk to the 'psst ahffice' (post office) to pick up the mail. As he was nearly deaf, he always asked the garage mechanics to set a wide gap on the car engine valve tappets so that he could hear the engine running.

Castle Hill Farm. Standing left to right: Uncle Sandy Morrison, Auntie Nance Morrison, Geoff Wheeler, Uncle Will Sharp, Dad; Seated from left to right: Joe Thompson ('Little' Joe), Dave, Aunty Alice Thompson, Nance, Geoff, and Mum - Marjorie Thompson. Photo by Esme Hadley.

NORTH COAST TRIP

Dad's upbringing made him a keen outdoors person, and prior to 1913 often had gone with old Minmi School mates on annual Christmas camping/fishing holidays of a few weeks on the Myall Lakes north of Newcastle. His Navy service interrupted these and in the early part of his marriage he tried to resume attending, leaving Mum and Dave and me with our grandparents at 'Glenroy'. However with the arrival of baby Nance, and then Joe, this arrangement was too one sided. At the end of 1930, the Morrisons were in great need of help, so we all spent the Christmas holiday break in their new home on the Castle Hill farm, doing lots of jobs. It was there on my 10th birthday that I received a 'walloping' from Dad, the reason long forgotten, but not Aunty Nance's consolation when they all realised what date it was - a rock cake and lemonade.

If there was any question of what to do next Christmas, it was resolved in about May 1931 when 'out of the blue' came to Mum an invitation from her old Fort Street Girls High School friend Eva Flower (nee Fraser in NZ) to spend a month with her at the cane/dairy farm at Condong on the Tweed River run by her husband Bob, during the next Christmas School holidays. We kids were included in the invitation and

Dad would be able to attend his Men's Camp. The cost of train travel was so high that a compromise scheme was worked out and quite exciting it sounded to me.

The scheme was for all of us to drive to Grafton in Overland, a trip of three or four days, with overnight accommodation for us to be in a tent at suitable roadside spots (camping grounds in those days were almost non-existent), then for us to go on to Murwillumbah by train, whilst Dad was to park the car in a garage in Grafton, return to Newcastle by train thence via Tea Gardens and launch to the Myall Lakes' camp. After the Men's camp was over Dad was to return to Grafton the same way, pick up the car and drive through to Condong via Murwillumbah.

Once our parents had agreed on the plan, the first thing to be done was to obtain a suitable tent. Cottage tents then were common but were not big enough for all of us, so Dad ordered an OSE Marquee tent 18 feet by 12 feet with walls 6 feet high, and with a 'Birkmyre' waterproof roof (an advanced feature then), from Hoseason and Coy, Ship Chandlers, of Sussex Street, Sydney.

While waiting for the tent to be made, Mum and Aunty Alice set to work on making six mattresses out of strong printed cotton material ('cretonne' they called it), 2 feet 3 inches in width and kapok filled, and with cross stitching every 12 inches, the end being 5 inches wider and twice as thick to act as a pillow. A sheet of black rubberised cloth (they called it 'American Cloth') was stitched on the edges (only) to act as a groundsheet, as the plan was for us to sleep on the ground under blankets.

As Overland now was 7 years old, this long trip called for serious preparation and Dad arranged for his Soccer mate, Jack Sansom (who by then was Head Mechanic of the wholesale grocery firm of Paterson, Laing and Bruce, in Sydney) to do the work in our garage, with Dad as 'labourer', at night time. Jobs to be done included fitting piston rings, and grinding the valves in the (side valve) engine, fitting new king pins and bushes and overhauling the steering box, and relining the external brake bands (footbrake). Jack was a powerfully built man of about 5 feet 8 inches in height who would save time in jacking the car by personally lifting the whole front of the car by levering his hands off his knees, enough for Dad to put timber chocks beneath the axle. I was an avid observer of all these activities, and genial Jack did not mind so long as I held the lamp on the end of the 'wandering lead' so that **he** could see what he was doing. In between times Dad took the opportunity to repaint the engine with heat resisting grey paint.

Dad also had made a tucker box with a hinged lid, out of timber, to fit on Overland's running board just below the doors, and bought an expanding lattice steel luggage rack which clamped on to the driver's side running board, to hold our big suitcases.

The new tent was delivered personally by Mr. Hoseason in his big blue Buick tourer. He was a stocky man in his late 50s, walked with a slightly rolling gait and had a thick Scandinavian accent to match. He evidently enjoyed dealing with someone like Dad who well knew seafaring things such as cordage and canvas. With its pungent scent the new acquisition was a great interest, and it was not long before Dad erected it as a trial on the back lawn - everything was there, poles, pegs and ropes.

School broke up on the second Thursday in December 1931 at about midday and Dad packed Overland, replacing the rear seat with the six tightly rolled up mattresses, clamped the luggage carrier on the driver's side running board and laid the tent in its canvas bag alongside the engine on the O.S., with the tent poles in their bag similarly laid on the opposite side. Mum was very busy packing the two big suitcases with clothes for us for the next six weeks, plus Christmas presents, not forgetting the Flowers.

Next morning we were all up at 4.30 am and after a snack, Dad stacked the suitcases on end behind the luggage carrier and held in by ropes; Mum filled the tuckerbox, and by 6 am. we were heading for Chatswood and the Pacific Highway. Our parents sat in front whilst in the back Dave sat behind Dad, I was behind Mum, and the babies Nance and Joe occupied the centre section between Dave and me. We kept to this arrangement for the whole trip.

The Pacific Highway from Hornsby to Kangaroo Point on the Hawkesbury River was paved with brand new cement concrete, smooth except for a bump at each black bitumen seal across the road at 50 foot intervals. We did not have to wait very long for the new diesel powered DMR ferry *Frances Peat*, which had been named after the wife of the man who first operated a ferry (sail powered) at this crossing. This one was a new Australian built sea going steel vessel which could hold about 20 cars, and had a central dividing structure supporting a 'bridge' at each end for the Captain. There were single lane ramps at each end of the ferry, lowered for access, and locked for safety during the 'voyage' of about 1½ miles to the north bank of the river.

Arriving there we found that the new Highway was paved with a reddish knobbly looking gravel and after about 5 miles Dad stopped for a roadside breakfast of Weetbix, grilled chops and toast, and tea, just at the start of a big sweeping right hand curve. Then on through Gosford where the gravel pavement was replaced by a bitumen surface through Ourimbah to Belmont where there was the start of concrete paving to Adamstown. We did not call at Newcastle but did call at The Hermitage, a fine old two storey home in Ballard Street, West Maitland, in which had lived since 1925 Mum's three maiden aunts. Here we also met their mother, our Great Grandmother Mary Scobie (nee Warren), a very alert 89 year old, although in a wheelchair. Aunty May was a schoolteacher (who had taught in Broken Hill), Aunty Mary who had stayed at home looking after her mother. Aunty 'Jen' (Janet) was blind, having lost her sight at the age of 6 years from the effects of a severe attack of whooping cough. All of our Aunts had most impressive noses, especially Aunty May who had a marvellous booming contralto voice to match.

It was well into the afternoon when we left The Hermitage; Dad started looking for a 'spot' for our camp as we neared the small town of Paterson, and soon after found a suitable site through a gate into a grassy paddock. There was no stock there so the grass was about three inches long, and looked comfortable after some small fallen branches were removed. The tent went up quickly, Dave and I being the helpers. Mum unrolled the mattresses and laid them with the line of 'pillows' at the centre, and made up beds with blankets. Dad made a fire for tea, after which he carefully drove Overland into the other half of the tent, with the tuckerbox facing the beds. In this our first **real** camp we soon went to sleep to the combined exciting scents of new canvas, crushed grass, motor car and gumleaves.

Before sunup next morning a family of magpies came around to investigate this intrusion and commented with carolling shouts, which soon woke us all. There was a heavy dew but Dad, (good bushman) had put dry wood and kindling under cover, and soon had a fire going for breakfast. By then the sun had risen properly and tent dried out in time for it to be packed last. Soon we were on our way into Dungog, a pretty little town surrounded by interesting looking hills, for food, and petrol for the car from a kerbside petrol 'bowser' in the main street, which had the first piece of bitumen surface since we left West Maitland. Soon it was back to the gravel road, and we turned off the main road at Dingadee, and headed for Weismantels through steep country. At a locality named Monkerai the road crossed the Karuah River, and Dad decided that this was a good place for us all to have a 'dip' to freshen up and wash away the dust. He had a shave, then we had an early lunch. The big timber truss bridge spanning the Karuah River, supported by what looked like whole tree trunks driven into the river bed, impressed me greatly.

Camp that night was a short distance north of Gloucester, a town overshadowed on the west by blocky hills, which I later learned were known as 'The Buckets'. We turned left off the Highway down a little side road leading to a fine running stream flanked by numerous sheoaks, which gave off a wonderful sighing sound in the evening breeze. The tent went up quickly and we had tea, then after it was properly dark, we all had a dip/wash in the creek having to be careful not to fall on the slippery round stones in the cool water.

Next morning Dad took the 'clean billy' to a dairy farm about 200 yards away on our side of the creek, and we had breakfast. This particular billy never was put on the fire, as were the other two billies, the big tinned steel frying pan and the open wire griller. Packing up after breakfast was much quicker - we were becoming experts! There was a certain difficulty in finding a suitable bush for toilet purposes but we managed in the nearby patch of scrub.

From Gloucester the gravelled Highway led up into the notorious 15 mile crossing of the Krambach Range, steep and with many blind bends. However we were spared the ultimate hazard of meeting a bullock team hauling a loaded timber 'jinker' on one of them, the only team we saw was resting on a level area off to the right of a comparatively straight section of Highway. Dad took it steadily and we arrived without incident at the village of Tinonee on the south bank of the Manning River. Here the gravelled Highway simply disappeared under the water, brakes needed to be working - there was no gate! While we were waiting a barge like ferry started coming across the river, hauling itself along a lone steel wire cable on the upstream side. This ferry could hold about 6 cars, this trip there were 3 plus a 1 ton truck. The ramp, being just above the water surface, rode up the stone paved approaches until the ferry stopped, someone on the ferry appeared to lock it to the cable, then the gate was opened, and the vehicles drove off past us. We then drove on, making 4 cars in all, the gate was closed and locked behind us and off we went. It was an eerie sensation to be in midstream of this big fast river dependent entirely upon the one cable as it rose from the muddy water in front of us, then vanished behind the ferry.

Taree was the biggest town we had seen since West Maitland and was full of bustling activity. Overland was filled with petrol (the filler cap was on top of the body in front of the driver), and on we went through a mixture of dairying country and heavy forest, crossing an interesting looking timber bridge, with a lift span in the centre, over the Camden Haven River. Equally interesting (to me at least) was a large rectangular timber punt in the river, fitted with a manually operated crane for lifting timber from local sawmills, and able to propel itself by a steam driven paddle wheel at rear - Dad called it a 'drogher'.

At the Hastings River just north of the turn-off to Port Macquarie, we crossed by another cable ferry - this time we felt safer, it was much bigger than that at Tinonee, and had two cables. Lunch was had on the north bank nearby, and we kids played on a tiny sandy beach on which the white sand graded upwards into almost black beneath the grass.

More forest awaited us after lunch and the 'babies' sharing the space in the rear seat often bored and boisterous, leading to dark threats from the front seat (never implemented it must be noted). Also the road surface deteriorated to a light coloured coarse sandy material, which had 'corrugated' (Dad's explanation) badly under traffic, requiring speeds of 40 miles per hour and more, to 'jump the tops.' Tyres on Overland had been upgraded to 'balloon' size at the rear (4½ inch section with 45 pounds per square inch pressure), and in the back we rode well. (However those at the front were the original 3½ inch section inflated to 60 pounds pressure, and as there were no shock absorbers anywhere on the car it was not safe to attempt 40 m.p.h. So we arrived at Kempsey with three broken leaves in the front pair of springs; one of these a main leaf which caused Dad quite some difficulty in steering the car.

We stayed there with Mum's cousin Lil Perrin (nee Scobie) and her two young daughters in their little cottage/shop. Dad next day had to find a blacksmith in town able to make the replacement spring leaves (which was the normal procedure in those days away from the city) and to fit them to Overland. Meanwhile at the shop which Lil ran, we kids must have been something of a nuisance, continually asking Mum for pennies to buy lollies.

Reassembling the springs had presented more difficulties than expected and we did not get going until after lunch on the following day, and late afternoon found us pitching the tent on the abandoned southern approaches to the original (demolished) bridge over Bonville Creek. Having the obligatory dip/swim in this creek was different, the water was brackish and light brown in colour, and there were lots of fallen logs on the bottom, all covered with slippery green slime.

Next morning Dad despatched Dave and me to the dairy farm about ¼ mile away on the other side of the (gravelled) Highway to have the clean billy filled for breakfast. Breaking camp had now become routine and on we went to Coffs Harbour, a large 'timber town' with an artificial harbour about a mile to the east near the Railway Station. It was here that we first saw bananas growing - there were acres of them on almost any hillside which faced easterly or north of easterly.

More gravelled Highway through partially developed country and we came to a village, Woolgoolga it was called; Dad said that it was an Aboriginal name, and it seemed that they made up most of the population. There was a sharp left hand bend in the centre of the village, then it was away in to forest again. It was not long before the road began to steadily worsen, ending in miles of roadworks under construction, and we travelled an appalling succession of rough side tracks which were deep in fine grey dust. This swirled into our open car, adding to the discomfort of a hot and humid day. We were glad when this was behind us and the last 20 miles into Grafton was on good gravel pavement, then bitumen from the outskirts to the brand new double decker road/rail bridge over the Clarence River, a **big** river. So new was this bridge that it had not been 'officially opened' (as I found out many years later) but there was no obstruction so Dad drove across into the City, then because so much time had been lost with broken springs, went straight to an hotel in the main street on the corner of Pound Street. There he hired a room for a couple of hours for us to have a clean up and to get ready for our afternoon train trip to Murwillumbah. This was an education for us kids, as we had come to believe that all that hotels did was 'to sell booze'.

Mum repacked clothes for herself and us kids into the two big suitcases, Dad travelled light with a smaller one, then drove us to the North Grafton Railway Station (until completion of the new bridge, the southern terminus of the Northern NSW system), and put us on the train standing there. Before long we were off, leaving Dad to park Overland in a garage next to 'our' hotel, then to take the night train back to Newcastle, thence to his Men's Camp on the Myall Lakes.

Our train trip was something of a trial to Mum as the day continued hot and muggy, so there was a steady demand for drinks from the Railway glass bottles in our compartment, and - in spite of their size, they were empty shortly after leaving Casino. The babies (Nan and Joe) were affected most, and were running around aimlessly 'like ants on a hot plate', as Mum put it. The only other occupant of our 8 seat compartment, obviously an experienced local traveller, saved the day by sharing his large bag of fresh fruit, and refused to accept any payment, or even give his name. Things got better after Byron Bay, when the train entered the afternoon shadows cast by the Burringbar Range - there was even the cool darkness of a tunnel. We were all relieved when the train pulled into Murwillumbah Station, and were able once more to set our feet on 'terra firma' (another of Dad's sayings). Bob and Eva Flower met us on the platform, and took us to their home near Condong, in his blue 1928 Buick tourer car.

This was a large corrugated iron roofed weatherboard house with 4 sizeable bedrooms, set on timber posts about 7 feet clear of the ground, and with a verandah all around, excepting on the south side. The house was separated from the Tweed River (not as big as Clarence River) by the Pacific Highway, and a single track railway leading to the Sugar Mill at Condong village about ¾ mile away to the east.

It was a genuine 'Queensland style' country home. There were big galvanised iron tanks to hold rainwater which was laid on to the kitchen and bathroom, but there was no electric power, so they used candles, in proper enamel candlesticks, except in the kitchen and the large living/dining room, where there were elegant, and very effective kerosene lamps. Later in our holiday I noticed lines of 3/16 inch diameter pipe running through the house, and other fittings on the ground floor, marked 'Petrolgas', I asked Bob Flower about it, his reply - 'Oh it was always giving trouble, and anyway, who needs bright lights'.

We quickly became friendly with their daughters Betty and Lois (the younger, about my age) and there was a lot to see around this 600 acre sugar cane and dairy farm, from the daily milking of more than 100 cows by machine to ploughing of paddocks to ready them for cane planting. One place was banned to us, the well from which water was pumped for washing etc., because it was open at the top, so, to help us keep our distance, Bob informed us that it was inhabited by a dangerous 'Go yow yow', no doubt a species of bunyip as I saw it. A large weeping willow not far from the house became a great attraction for us kids, until a limb gave way under Dave's weight and he fell 8 feet to the ground, breaking his left arm, necessitating a visit to a doctor in Murwillumbah; he called it a 'greenstick break', but it still had to be bound up firmly.

Bob Flower was generous with his time and his car, and we went with him and his family on several picnics, including one to Cudgen Beach, on the way passing villages on the banks of the Tweed River with names like Chinderah and Tumbulgum, each with equally interesting (to me at least) 2 car ferries on which a single cylinder Petrol engine drew the ferry across the river by a single steel cable. On one of these picnics we actually crossed into Queensland and had a surf at their southern-most beach - Kirra was its name - which was practically deserted, we almost had it to ourselves.

Our wonderful holiday within sight of Mount Warning at last came to an end and so did Dad's Men's Camp. He returned to Grafton by train, picked up Overland from the garage, crossed the new bridge again to get to the Pacific Highway, which he then followed to the north. Bob Flower drove us about 5 miles out of Murwillumbah hoping to meet him, but Dad had headlight trouble at Mooball, and had to stay the night there for repairs next day, then came on in the daylight. Bob Flower was emphatic that to cross the Burringbar Range at night was far safer because headlights gave advance warning on the numerous blind bends.

After a day for Dad to recover, Overland was again fully packed, and we bade farewell to the Flower family, the Tweed River and old Mount Warning, and set out along the Highway through 'the Burringbar.' The pavement throughout was gravel, and the road was every bit as bad as 'The Krambach'; blind hairpin bends abounded some on steep 'pinches', and all in heavily forested steep mountain country. Dad had just gone over it a few days before, and we had no trouble at all. Mum had a cousin she always referred to as 'Minnie' (nee Mary Warren Kerr) who had married a bank officer named McLennan who later had turned to dairy farming near Mullumbimby, at Wilson's Creek. Their farm was not far out of our way so we turned off the main road and stayed with them for a 'cuppa' and to meet our cousins. They introduced us to the Australian Bush Nut (Macadamia) of which they had half a dozen growing native on the farm. The nuts had a very hard shell, requiring a hammer to get to the kernel, but that was well worth the effort, it was delicious.

Then on to Lismore, a big bustling town on the banks of the Richmond River, which we crossed by a timber truss bridge. It was now getting late in the day, and the dairy country offered little in the way of suitable camping 'spots'; we had to make do with a site on the Casino Road on the banks of a small clear creek, with the railway in front of us, and the main road 150 yards to the rear. It was not very private, but with tent pitched, and after dark, Dad was able to shepherd us into the shallow water of the creek for a 'dip' to wash off the dust.

We slept well and after breakfast, broke camp and headed off for Casino, also on the Richmond River, which we crossed by another timber truss bridge then turned west through a small village - Mummulgum was its name, sounded aboriginal to us, then tackled the steep and winding climb over the Richmond Range. It was not as tough as 'the Burringbar', but it was steep, and Overland's engine had to work its hardest since the overhaul, and there was a strong smell of hot paint. Nevertheless it did not miss a beat, and with these other mountain crossings behind him, Dad handled this one with confidence. Then it was over the top and a long descent into the valley of the Clarence River and a pretty little village - Mallanganee. All over this range there were lots of grass trees, which Dad called 'blackboys', growing close to the roadside.

The next town Tabulam, was the biggest since Casino, and was on the east bank of the Clarence River, which although miles upstream from Grafton, evidently was a big stream in flood time, because a large timber truss bridge had been necessary to span it; after the Karuah Bridge I was taking note of bridges. It seemed that most of the population of Tabulam was aboriginal.

Steady climbing through hilly timbered country brought us to an old mining village with the name Drake (I thought of the drakes at Castle Hill farm which used to attack me), situated on a little flat next to a creek. As we came into the village a sudden thunderstorm hit us, and started dropping hailstones the size of pigeon eggs. It was fortuitous that Drake still boasted a blacksmith, and that we happened to be near his double fronted shed the right hand side of which was empty. The smith waved Dad in to take shelter - the din on the corrugated iron roof was terrific for about 20 minutes, then it was all over except for soft light rain. Dad thanked the blacksmith who was very interested to learn that we were tourists from Sydney, quite a rarity in his village.

From here on the road started the serious business of climbing the Great Dividing Range, and wound its way up and up through steep timbered country, finally to emerge on to a plateau, which increasingly was cleared as we approached Tenterfield, a pretty bustling town surrounded by cleared paddocks, and overshadowed by a big mountain to the west. It was getting late so after buying petrol and food in town, Dad headed Overland south on the (gravel paved) New England highway, until he found a 'spot' for the camp about 2 miles south of Tenterfield, a short distance down a side road east of the Highway at Bungulla Gap. This site was not very exciting (no creek), but there were bushes for shelter, and plenty of fallen sticks for the fire, so after pitching the tent and having a meal (Mum had become very adept at creating a meal out of the tuckerbox), we all slept well in our beds, too tired to care about the hard ground.

The following day was fine and clear, there was no dew and packing up was done quickly - we older boys were able to be useful helpers to Dad by now. The Highway climbed for a few miles then over a gap at a village named Bungulla, and descended past a huge rock mass called Bluff Rock, which Dad said probably was the core of an ancient volcano, all very quiet now even in the tiny village and railway station at its foot. This country looked different from the coast; the soil seemed to be very gritty, and there were numerous large rounded boulders (Dad said they were granite) strewn about the paddocks, and as far as I could see, well in to the bush. There was a substantial climb up the Bolivia Range, but Dad took it in his stride, and before long we came to Deepwater, a busy little town which, Dad said, had originally been centre of a tin mining activity. We did not stop, but pushed on and more climbing to another and higher level of the plateau and through to Glen Innes.

This was a **real** town, with big buildings and shops, but we did not have time to spare, so it was buy petrol, and be on our way. I had noticed a change to a rich looking volcanic soil as we entered this town, and it continued through to the next much smaller town, Guyra was its name, after more climbing for Overland. There was an interesting looking natural lake immediately west of the town - the map called it the 'Mother of Ducks Lagoon', and was unusual being located next to what turned out to be the highest town on the whole trip. From here it was a steady descent to Armidale, which was a really fine town, complete with big churches and public buildings, Dad said that they often had snow in winter. Outside Armidale we came upon great granite boulders in the paddocks again, and it was more descending to a small town called Bendemeer where Dad found a good camping 'spot' in a public reserve on the banks of the McDonald River just ¼ mile north of an interesting timber truss bridge which carried the New England Highway over the river into the town's main street.

It was a good 'spot', there was grass on which to pitch the tent, and public toilets nearby. We were all glad of a dip/wash in the river alongside us, although it was quite chilly. We kids were a little sad as we could see that almost certainly this was going to be our last camp, as Dad had announced that the next day's stop would be at the home of his sister 'Jinny' (Jane Sharp) in Newcastle. So we went off to sleep in our 'roll-up' beds to the sound of the river bubbling over smooth stones, sensing that this trip had been something of an achievement - Dad kept reminding us that 'all good things come to an end'.

Next morning there was a heavy dew, but Dad could not wait until the sun had dried the tent completely as we still had a long way to go, and in any case heavy clouds ahead promised rain, so we packed a damp tent. About twenty minutes after leaving little Bendemeer light rain started to fall, and set in heavily just as we commenced the steep descent of the notorious Moonbi Range. With all this mountain experience behind him Dad simply put Overland into second gear for both of these steep and winding descents, and kept his brakes in reserve; we had no trouble at all.

The gravel pavement on the Highway gave way to a pleasant smooth bitumen surface as we entered Tamworth, and Dad pointed out the power station on the right hand side, which had given this city electric power before any other Australian country town. Further in there were numerous public buildings and a large well established shopping centre. We did not stop but pushed on over a large timber bridge which spanned the Peel River almost in the middle of the town.

The bitumen ended at the outskirts of town and it was on through open rolling cleared wheat country of what Dad called the 'Liverpool Plains', firstly through a village with a signboard 'Goonoo Goonoo'; Dad said that it was a private town, and that its aboriginal name correctly was pronounced 'Gunna Gunnoo'; I was amazed. This fine plateau country continued, with a descent to the village of Wallabadah, then on to Willowtree, after which a substantial mountain range loomed up ahead, from which a stream emerged, and the Highway (still gravel paved) followed its valley to a tiny village named Ardglen. Here we crossed the railway at a level crossing, then Dad put Overland into second gear for the very sharp ascent ahead of what he said was the Liverpool Range. All went well in second gear until about half way up, the road suddenly became really steep, causing the engine to labour and me to become more than apprehensive, then quick as a flash Dad whipped Overland down into rst gear and we crawled to the top; it was the steepest 'pinch' of this whole trip. This steep pinch south from Ardglen apparently caused several accidents and caused the DMR to construct a deviation in 1935-36 which had easier grades.

From the top of the Range we had an excellent view of a fine valley, into which we descended in second gear - it was not so steep this side. In the valley floor we entered a town with another aboriginal name - Murrurundi, which straddled the Pages River, which Dad said was the major tributary of the Hunter River. So it seemed that from here on everything was comparatively 'civilized'; there was smoke coming out of a mountain on the east side of the Highway at one place, Mount Wingen Dad said was its name, and was **not** a volcano, but a coal seam which had been set alight years ago where it came to the surface, probably by a bushfire.

On through Scone a very tidy town with one long main street like Murrurundi, then Muswellbrook with a steep main street and scary (to me at least) underpass bridge beneath the railway. We had, previous to Muswellbrook at a small town named Aberdeen, crossed the Hunter River over a fine lattice steel truss bridge, and it was not until we came to Singleton that we crossed this big river for the last time, and followed its west bank into West Maitland. The Highway went right through the main street which was lined with many prosperous looking shops, although Dad said that it was under flood level. We did not stop at 'The Hermitage', but pushed on through East Maitland (which Dad said was a Government planned town and above flood level) to Newcastle, and to the home of Aunty Jinny and Uncle Will Sharp, and our cousin Edna at 122 Lindsay Street, Hamilton.

In the excitement of our arrival Dave forgot Dad's rule **not** to get out of the car on the driver's side, caught his foot in a rope and fell heavily on to the roadway, opening up the break in his left arm again. This necessitated a visit to a local Doctor, who turned out to be Idris Morgan, an old schoolmate of Dad's from Minmi Public School. The car was parked outside Sharp's for the night, which we spent on our mattress beds all made up on the floor of their lounge room. Aunty Jinny made us very welcome; she was an excellent cook, and we were happy to tuck into her generous tasty meals.

After all the happenings of the previous 6 weeks, the trip back to Willoughby next day was something of an anti-climax, even including the crossing of the Hawkesbury River, this time by the twin vessel the *George Peat*. But it was good to be home again in familiar surroundings, even though these included lawns to be mown and gardens weeded. Our 'Perdriau' tyres had given no trouble at all, not even a puncture.

A few days later, on the following Tuesday (early February 1932) I went with Dad in Overland to North Sydney Boys High School and enrolled in 1st Year; the Headmaster was Mr. William Williams, and the Sportsmaster/P.T. Man was Mr. William Elliott. I was 11 years and 1 month old.

The School building was a substantial 2 story brick structure on the south side of Falcon Street. A long wing of classrooms went out from the south-east corner, making a quadrangle at the western side of which was a tuck shop run by the Aldersons, who had a pastry cook business around the corner in Miller Street. Our school colours were Chocolate and Pink, In the quadrangle Mr Elliot led us all in twenty minutes of P.T. at weekly intervals, standing at the mid-level of the outside staircase. To our surprise after about 3 weeks the Aldersons without explanation and management of the tuck shop put in the hands of Mrs Winney and started "home cooking" in the shop. A big change.

On 16 March 1932 all classes were cancelled and the whole school assembled in North Sydney Park in fours for marching and, led by Mr Elliot, moved to Miller Street towards the new Bridge which we crossed together with several thousand other school groups from the North Shore. There was a light drizzle but it was an event for us school kids in advance of the official opening the following Saturday 19th March.

Back at the School in the next few weeks our new headmaster announced that the school colours in the future would be Bismark (Brown) and Coral (Pink), and that the school badge was to be redesigned to accepted Heraldic Rules that required a third colour, which was to be Gold. This caused some resentment among older pupils. Dad referred to the whole episode as BUSYNARK AND QUARREL. Another change he told us about at home was that his two soccer teams were to be abolished. In front of the whole school at lunch, Dad confronted Mr Harvey and persuaded him to change his mind.

*First and second panels of the Sydney Harbour Bridge,
becoming the first big span when closed up; started 5th
September 1929, Southern end. Photograph by Albert
Mitchell, courtesy Richard Lloyd.*

SYDNEY
HARBOUR BRIDGE

While we were still in Mudgee (as I learned much later the 'turning of the first sod' for the new bridge over Sydney Harbour took place on a very wet Saturday afternoon 28th July 1923, at the corner of Blue and Miller Streets, North Sydney.

We did not become fully aware of this big engineering project until we moved into our new home at 102 Lyle Street, East Willoughby after which Dad often used to take us in Overland to 'Glenroy' to visit our Grandparents. To get there from Willoughby the most direct route was to take a vehicular ferry across the Harbour to the City, then travel Victoria Road through to Rozelle and to Tilba Avenue, Balmain. On the City side there was only one terminus for these ferries and this was alongside the Fort Macquarie Tram Sheds, present site of the Opera House, but on the north side there were two termini, one at the foot of Miller Street at McMahon's Point, the second at Milson's Point, which had been moved easterly around to Jeffrey Street to make way for the large workshops set up by the Bridge Contractors, Dorman Long and Company, an English firm (now the site of Luna Park and North Sydney Olympic Pool).

Whichever one Dad took, the trip across the Harbour gave an excellent view of the activities on the Bridge, and the air was full of the insistent sound of pneumatic hammers driving home, as Dad said, the hundreds of red hot steel rivets needed to stitch together the whole structure. It was fascinating to me to see the two arch halves grow out from the shores suspended by great bunches of thick steel cable which Dad said were anchored deep in tunnels cut down into solid sandstone well behind the ends of the arch support Main bearings - there were two of these on each side of the Harbour.

The passenger ferries of course were still in full operation and whenever we went 'to Town' we would take the tram to Milson's Point passenger terminal, from which we would pass beneath the great arms of the Bridge as they reached towards each other, on our way to Circular Quay. At last the two ends were only a few inches apart, a rumour spread that erroneously the western gap was less than the eastern, but it was only the effect of the setting sun, next morning they were the same. Finally on Wednesday 20th August 1930 after careful slackening of the support cables and placing of two large steel locking pins to guide the ends, they came together late at night, it was supporting itself as a three hinged arch. As I learned years later, there was much to be done to complete the top chords of the arch, they were in place within a week, then on 8th September, under light fleecy cloud cover, four powerful hydraulic jacks forced the top chords apart, with a load of 3248 tons, and while this was held the arch was finally closed up, becoming a two hinged arch. This stage of the original and daring engineering undertaking was complete, and all of Sydney felt a sense of achievement; the sceptics were silenced.

Now it was the second stage for us to watch from the ferries, as long steel hangers were brought out on barges from the Workshops at Milson's Point (as had every part of the arch itself) and lifted into position by the creeper cranes, and secured against swaying by ropes from the arch above. A fabricated steel cross girder, which would be the support for the roadway, was lifted by the two cranes, and the bottom ends of the hangers threaded into slots, and fixed by 16 inch diameter steel pins.

The sound of riveting still went on, but much subdued now that the arch had been completed, and our attention was gripped now by the new deck which was taking shape in the midspan, and working outward finally to reach the ends of the arch span in 1931, and being completed, along with a host of other big jobs on the approach spans and tunnels while we were absent on our trip to Murwillumbah.

By February 1932 the whole of the work on the new Bridge was finished, and it was time for the engineers to load test the structure. This was done by shunting a total of 96 old steam locomotives and 46 tenders onto the rail tracks on each side of the bridge, which I found out later, was a total load of 8280 tons. The engineers checked deflections with various combinations of positions of this load, moved as needed, and gave their O.K. Under political pressure from Councils on the North Shore the rail tracks on the eastern side of the Bridge were converted to carry trams right into the new Wynyard Station, then, on Wednesday 16th March, 10,000 School children (including me) from Schools within a 10 mile radius of the Bridge, were marched across the new roadway, and then back **again.** It was drizzling rain, but we were all pleased to have taken part in another 'test'.

On the following Saturday, 19th March 1932, the Bridge was formally opened at the southern end by the Premier, Mr. Jack Lang after an unsuccessful attempt to forestall him by a uniformed Army Officer on horseback, wielding a sword, one Captain de Groot, an active member of the New Guard movement which regarded Mr. Lang as a dangerous radical. Dad had taken us all in Overland to a vantage point opposite North Sydney Post Office, where we had an excellent view of the great procession as it came up the rise after crossing the Bridge, a momentous day. To cap it all, trams from Willoughby started running into Wynyard Station that afternoon, as did trains from Hornsby. After all the excitement died down, there was the continuing interest in being able to **walk** into the City, on either of the two footways; certainly it was a long way, but it was free! Suddenly the ferries looked forlorn, they had little to do now.

A motion picture record of the Bridge construction had been made in three versions, on 16mm film by the Manager of Harringtons Photo Store in George Street, a Mr. Henri Mallard, who shot about 2000 feet of film on a 16mm silent Bell & Howell spring action 3 lens camera, light enough to be hand-held. Two variant 35mm editions exist, one being made for public exhibition. This took place in April at the Prince Edward Theatre, but because of lack of interest, and competition from the new talking picture 'The Singing Fool', it was only screened half a dozen times. Dad took us all to **hear** Al Jolson sing at the Capitol Theatre. This 35mm print was photographed mainly on 35mm silent film by Paramount, with some additions clearly by enlargement from Mallard's 16mm movie, became the property of the Department of Main Roads, where years later in 1956, I was fortuitously able to avert its destruction for reasons of fire hazard; and is now in the National Film Archive in Canberra.

Durras Inslet with Point Upright in the background, 1934.

DURRAS

As the winter of 1932 came, our thoughts turned to next year's holiday. It was obvious to me from remarks Dad made to Mum that he was most disappointed with the 1931/32 Men's Camp which it appeared had turned into what he referred to as an 'expensive booze' party (there were **cases** of whisky and gin) during which, as the only sober member, he was expected to cook for them all, so he had determined never to go to another.

A friend of Dad's from his Newcastle days, Jack Towns, who lived near the Pennant Hills Railway Station and taught Science at Sydney Boys' High School, suggested that we camp at a seaside property owned by his late wife's people, north of Batemans Bay, the name sounded like 'Duris', but was spelled 'Durass'. As Mum had taken to camping like a 'duck to water', she was soon persuaded, after all it was only necessary to find a 15 foot by 12 foot tarpaulin to make a 'dining room,' and fishing gear for us. We kids needed no persuading.

A new tarpaulin would have been too expensive, so Mum improvised one out of pieces of heavy canvas from discarded industrial filters, found by Aunty Nance, and sewn together on Mum's treadle sewing machine, which being a heavy duty type, could cope with this material; then Dad hand sewed eyelets for ropes along the 12 foot edges. He also got to work making telescopic fishing rods from a fine grained tough timber he called 'greenheart', and bought a secondhand Browning 0.22 calibre 'trombone repeater' rifle from a shop in Willoughby Road, Crows Nest; also some ammunition.

Dad's brother Robert was a Senior Officer in the NSW Railways, closely involved with detailed investigation of major accidents. He and Aunty Lily lived with our cousins Marjorie and Ken in Correys Avenue Concord. While on holidays on 16 March 1933, he and Aunty Lily, returning from a visit to Taronga Park Zoo, caught a train at Town Hall, when without warning he collapsed in the train as it was coming out of tunnel, and died at Central Station, where the train was delayed to attend to him. Uncle Bob was only 47 years of age and his death was a great shock to Dad, whose only other brother in communication with the family, was Uncle William, who was much older; he lived at Cessnock. Aunty Nance, Aunty Alice and Dad tried to be of help to the Concord Thompsons at this sad time. Weeks later, back at Willoughby, Dad decided not to cancel the arrangements made with Jack Towns for us to go camping at Durras.

School broke up on the second Thursday in December 1932, and by bedtime Overland had been packed similarly to the North Coast trip. Next morning at 4.30 a.m. found us all up, and after a bite to eat, and final packing, Dad drove us over the new Bridge, through the quiet City, on through Newtown, past St. Peter's Church of England with its incredibly slender spire supports, to cross the George's River at Tom Ugly's Point, by a new steel bridge. The bitumen pavement ended just south of Sutherland, near the terminus of the steam tram from Cronulla - we even saw one of those! The Prince's Highway from here on was paved with a reddish gravel, but it was in good order. At 8 o'clock after 2 hours on the road, it was time for breakfast so Dad turned off into a small cleared spot just north of the side road to Helensburgh; we appreciated the Weetbix, grilled chops and Billy tea.

The bitumen pavement started again at the top of Bulli Pass, and Dad slipped into second gear to make this notorious descent, even so there was smoke coming from the brakes by the time we had reached the foot of the hill. Then it was on into Wollongong through little coal mining towns which Dad often used to refer to as sources of good Soccer footballers, Woonona, Corrimal and Balgownie.

We called for lunch at the home of Dad's eldest sister, who always was addressed as 'Poll', although her real name was Mary. She was married to Uncle Sid Gow, a big bluff man with reddish hair, who obviously was a very competent carpenter, to judge from the stylish house he had built here at 56 Atchison Street, and the incredible inlaid dining table he had made with 8 matching chairs. We were glad to meet some new cousins.

The sealed pavement on the Highway stopped at the western end of Crown Street then it was gravel again all the way to Kiama over numerous timber bridges including a big truss bridge over the Minnamurra River. The country was becoming more open with many dairy cows grazing in the rolling paddocks. Tiny trains hauled by steam engines fitted with spark arrester type funnels, chuffed up and down the main streets of Kiama on narrow gauge tracks, bringing crushed bluemetal from quarries above the town to a wharf in the sheltered little harbour. Dad pointed out a small rusty red ship with the name 'Bombo', which was loading bluemetal for transport to Sydney.

We turned up a side road leading to Kiama Hospital, and just beyond it found Love's old farmhouse 'Silver Hill', where Mum had spent holidays as a child; Grandpa Roberts had been Headmaster of Kiama Public School at the turn of the century. One of the sons, Paddy Love, was now running the farm, and his sister Gwen, who always was referred to as 'Eggy', kept house for him. He was good company for us kids, full of jokes like:

'Ever heard the story of the three wells? You didn't ?
Well, well, well.'

We spent the night on our mattresses on the floor of the sitting room of 'Silver Hill' to the combined interesting scents of homemade soap, a wood fuel stove in the kitchen and a fresh sea breeze.

Next day the Highway wound tortuously through steep hillsides to a long descent to a tiny Railway Station with the name 'Omega'. This seemed familiar to me as it was here that Mum, Dave, Nance, Joe and I had got off the train from Sydney to spend the 1927 Christmas holidays with the Loves at their other farm 'Taballa' in Rose Valley, whilst Dad went to his Men's Camp. We crossed the Railway at Omega then the Highway followed low lying swampy ground before climbing sharply to the village of Gerringong on the top of a prominent hill; a pretty spot with numerous large trees in the streets - Dad called them 'Norfolk Island Pines'. Except for short stretches of bitumen here and there at villages, the gravelled Highway took us right into Bomaderry, which Dad said was the end of the Railway - we continued across a large steel lattice bridge over the Shoalhaven River, wide and deep, into Nowra itself.

Here we were introduced to the 'CWA' - the Country Womens Association, as it was in their rooms that we met Mrs Judy Brown (nee Love from Kiama) and her dairy farmer husband, Alec, and had lunch with them. They had come into Nowra especially to meet us, from their farm at Cambewarra, west of here. Nowra impressed me as a fine bustling town, but seemed too far inland to get much of a cooling sea breeze.

The gravelled pavement started again just south of Nowra and took us through timbered hilly country to the village of Tomerong, which a signboard announced to be Headquarters of the Clyde Shire Council. There were busy sawmills at another village sprawled along the Highway, its name was Wandandian, had to be aboriginal. After passing the turnoff to Lake Conjola, the road descended to what a signboard said was Boolgatta Flat, the soil was almost black and looked very fertile. At the southern end there was a tiny settlement with another aboriginal name - Yatte Yattah. Dad stopped at a cheese factory on the eastern side of the Highway, and came back with a 'half cheese', which weighed 14 pounds, it was a pale orange in colour, with a marvellous aromatic scent which soon filled the car.

About a mile south of the cheese factory a side road led off to the right to the settlement of Croobyar, where Grandpa Roberts had told me that he had been born, in the Schoolhouse, where his father had been the Head Teacher. Grandpa also had described to me the trip when he was a boy, by bullock wagon to Glen William on Williams River, north of Newcastle, after his father had been transferred - it took five weeks Grandpa said, over the Christmas holidays.

Narrawallee Creek was crossed by an unusual timber bridge - it was built on a right hand curve on an up grade of about 1 in 20. I had never seen one like it. Then there was a sudden steep ascent to Milton, announced by a big sign:

> 'Welcome to Milton
> A Good Rexona Town'.

The first two words were replaced by the word 'Farewell' on the reverse side, for the benefit of northbound travellers; there were numerous similar signs at other towns. Milton was a proper town, set on a prominent rise, with established stores, a Police Station, a Hospital, Court House and Churches built of stone, and the main street was sealed, but we had to move on.

More gravel road led through forest past a turnoff with a DMR sign 'Molymoke' (years later changed to Mollymook by Mum's friend Alison Clissold when she was subdividing her land there) and then it was a timber bridge over Millards Creek, with a big sawmill on the right hand side, into the seaside village of Ulladulla set on the western edge of a small natural coastal inlet. There were a few fishing boats in the little harbour, plus what Dad referred to as a ship of the Illawarra and South Coast Steam Navigation Company, tied up alongside the small stone wharf projecting from the beach, the ship's tall funnel was quite distinctive. The village was dominated by the 'chuff chuff' sound of a big single cylinder steam engine in the sawmill as it took the load of the whining 6 foot diameter circular saws biting into a hardwood log.

Several miles of scrubby country brought us over a hill and down to a village built on the edge of a swamp, Burrill Lake (pronounced B'reel as we learned later) named after the lake alongside, which was open to the sea; we crossed by another timber bridge, then it was more forest country to a long stretch of Highway (gravelled) between sandhills on the east side, and swamp along the edge of another lake. It too was open to the sea, the sign at the timber bridge which carried us across the entrance said it was Lake Tabourie, but further on another sign said Lake Toubouree - these aboriginal names present difficulties to Europeans it seems. Both of these lakes looked inviting, but Dad said 'swamps breed mosquitoes'.

Termeil turned out to be a tiny village serving a cattle grazing area, and was the start of 15 miles of very winding road over the notorious (as we later learned) Cockwhy Range. No part of this road was very steep, but abounded in sharp curves, many of them quite 'blind', which were something of a hazard from the 7 seater Studebaker and Buick sedan service cars, whose drivers knew the speed rating of every bend between Nowra and Bega. However with Krambach, Burringbar and Moonbi Ranges behind him, Dad kept us out of trouble.

East Lynne we found to be a busy little sawmill village surprisingly located in heavy forest on the western end of a lake, where a drogher (punt) would carry south coast timber back and forth. The sawmill of course was driven by a large steam engine which sounded like that at Ulladulla; on the opposite (western) side stood a timber Post Office/ Store, with several timber cottages for company. Years later in 1940 the DMR relocated the Highway and part of this village was moved, but not the sawmill.

Several miles further on we came upon another sawmill village, the DMR sign said 'Benandra', about ½ mile south of a road leading off to the left - its sign read 'Durras Lake'; so that was the correct spelling: Benandra itself was a cut above East Lynne having a proper nicely painted School, its name was 'Benandarah', and in addition to a large steam driven sawmill west of the Highway, had a 10 foot square corrugated iron Post Office - its name was 'Benanderah'. I preferred the DMR version. There were several timber cottages within walking distance of the sawmill.

The Durras road left the Highway at an angle which favoured traffic from the south, immediately crossed a creek, passing a large timber two storey barn on the left then a roomy cottage, and quickly became little more than a two wheeled track through the dense forest, in which spotted gums took pride of place in numbers alongside stringybarks and blackbutts, with an occasional ironbark. At one place the track sidled steeply under a small cliff into a deep gully smelling aromatically; Dad said that the small trees with distinctive leaves were the source, and were called 'Myrtles.' Across the little creek (dry at the time) then it was up a steep pinch to the top of a timbered ridge, and if we thought that was steep, the next descent capped it. Dad dropped Overland into 1st gear, even so the rear wheels slid on the loose gravelly track so that we narrowly missed a large spotted gum growing close to the track on the driver's side.

Before long we came upon dozens of low growing palms amongst the big trees, with shiny dark green leaves - Dad called them 'burrawongs', and the closer we came to the coast the thicker they were growing. A few more hills and we came down to a swampy flat densely timbered with tall sheoaks, and the road was carried across on sawn hardwood planks about 5 inches thick by 12 feet in length, laid crossways and held down by other similar planks laid longitudinally, secured with fencing wire at intervals. It was rough travelling, but the only way to get across this boggy black soil flat; Dad called it a 'corduroy'.

Out of the swamp through heavy sliprails (my job to move them), across a small ti-tree flat on reddish soil, and we drove up a grassy slope to a large rambling timber house on the left, with lots of verandahs and a corrugated iron roof. A tall man came from a side entrance to greet us, this was Mr. Jack Towns, and the big home was the one in which his late wife had been brought up as a girl; the family name was McMillan. I noticed that there were other cottages not far away, also some sheds.

Jack Towns was a tall powerfully built man, as could be expected from his younger days as a champion sculler; he spoke with a husky rumbling voice in a genial manner, and was very pleased to see us - visitors from Sydney were not usual. He personally led us down to the area of the property where we were to camp, at two shillings and sixpence per week. The track went through sliprails, then wound down through a forest of big trees from which it seemed to me that many larger trees had been taken in the past for milling. The track then opened out into a clearing near the southwestern end of a big bay, which had a very prominent cliff at the northern end about 2 miles away. At the extreme southern end there was a small rocky island not far off-shore. There were literally miles of beautiful beaches, we kids could see endless possibilities.

However it was late in the day, and Dave and I were summoned to help Dad with the immediate task of putting up the tent, in a grassy spot behind the sand dunes, with a few big trees for company. It was almost dark when this was completed and no doubt caused to be over-looked a nest of very angry black 'bull joe' ants (about 1 inch in length) right under the mattress beds laid on the grass. They brought con-siderable pain and confusion in the dark tent, just as we were getting ready to sleep. By the light of a hurricane lamp and our only torch, all bedding was taken apart and shaken, and the several bites treated by Mum with Eichorn's Remedy. Dad located the nest and administered discouragement in the form of a gallon of boiling water. After the beds were remade we all slept soundly to the gentle rumble of surf, alongside Overland which occupied one half of the tent as usual.

Next day was very busy. Armed with his new 3½ pound American 'Plumb' axe, Dad went into the forest about ¼ mile away and cut down 12 saplings for the sides of the bunks made of two wheat bags sewn open end to open end, which we had brought down from Willoughby. Then from a couple of older fallen trees he cut two heavier trunks to support the 12 saplings, then cut 4 solid tree forks, to support these two, by being set in the ground. Dave and I were kept at it all day carrying the saplings and forks, and helping Dad fabricate the bunks by threading the smaller saplings through holes cut in the bottoms of the wheat bags, so that they could be stretched apart, then secured to the heavier trunks with 4 inch nails. The whole job was done before dark, enabling Mum to make up our mattress beds on the stretched wheat bags, and above ground. On the following day Dave and I were nearly as busy helping Dad obtain more saplings for the dining room, and building a hole-in-the-ground toilet, surrounded by ti-tree walls, about 70 yards away.

Dad made a 'permanent' fireplace a few yards from the dining room, using rocks lying about; the meat safe was suspended from the ridge pole of the dining room, the cheese was kept in this. Jack Towns brought down a 44 gallon drum of rainwater for us, for drinking; he and Dad set it on a couple of short logs shaped to fit. A few days later Dad went for a walk on the beaches and came back with enough driftwood to make a rough table 5 feet by 2½ feet, plus benches for us to sit on.

At first Dad fished from nearby Caines Rocks and the beaches either side: then on the advice of Jack Mahony who was camped not far from us and had been coming to Durras for years to fish for groper, tried various spots on the point at the southern end of the Bay, called Mill Point near the presence of a large disused sawmill, almost complete, on the northern side. Later Dad ventured further south to the next point which was separated from the land by a 3 foot wide gap (an ancient volcanic dyke, Dad said) and accessed through a natural archway, broken at the top by this gap. The Archway we always called it, and it provided good fishing.

Dad introduced me to the rifle and was most careful to impress on me the safety aspects first; then how to shoot rabbits - never shoot at **what looks like** a rabbit, you must see its eyes, etc. I afterwards found that bagging a rabbit was only the first step; skinning and cleaning it ready for cooking was something less exciting.

Dad soon got us into a routine of going fishing early (after a snack) then coming back to camp about 11 am for a dip/wash in the surf, and breakfast. This became known in the family as 'Brunch', with tea before sundown as all cooking was done at the open fireplace. Thus there were two proper meals each day which were very adequate for us, except on one occasion when brother Joe (6 years) who was learning to count at School, worked out, just as he was going to bed, that he had only had two meals that day, and insisted upon a token third in the form of a large slice of bread and jam (Mum had made big tins of plum jam at Willoughby, and brought them with us).

That year Jack Towns, well before our arrival had planted about a quarter of an acre each of onions and tomatoes, and the season had been very good. Hence there was a more than adequate supply, we even learned to eat really ripe tomatoes like an apple. Dad introduced us to a favourite camp dish of his, onions sliced up and browned in dripping in the frying pan, then tomatoes were sliced in and cooked lightly, with gratings of cheese, the whole 'solidified' with 4 or more hen eggs. Delivered to a piece of toast we made by the side of the fire, it was irresistible - Dad called it 'Squnce'.

There were about five other camps in the area plus some families occupying a cottage back from the beach and another on Mill Point near the old sawmill. Jack Mahony was a horse racing man whose specialty was groper, which he sought with enthusiasm and heavy cord lines on strong rods. On one occasion he caught a 25 pound blue groper and shared a lot of it with us - good eating although a trifle coarse. His son Geoff and I became friends, but this was to be Mahony's last Durras; Jack told Dad that 'it was getting too civilized'.

Dad drove us into Bateman's Bay a few times to buy petrol, groceries and a newspaper (our mail was delivered to Towns' house). The Clyde River was wide, and deep enough for the I.& S.C.S.N. Coy vessels to tie up at a wharf right in town; we crossed by a steam powered DMR ferry which had two steel cables connected to the land. On the south shore just west of the ferry landing, was a large sawmill with what must have been a two cylinder steam engine, as its exhaust was less emphatic; this mill had its own wharf fronting the River, to which ocean going vessels could tie up to load sawn timber. The town itself was about 3 blocks in length spread along the Princes Highway which was sealed with bitumen from the ferry to a mile south at the outskirts. There was a Hotel, Post Office, Police Station, Baghursts NRMA garage, and a couple of little timber Churches; it was quite a centre which also included a substantial general store run by a Mrs E.Thomsen, widow of a Scandinavian seafaring man; we obtained most of our requirements here. The nearest Hospital was at Milton, back over the Cockwhy.

The daily round of events at 'The Bay' started with the swift arrival of the big service cars from Narooma and Bega; it was a short stop to pick up passengers and Mail, then over the ferry and up the gravel Highway on the north side in a flurry of dust on their way to meet the midday train from Sydney at Bomaderry. After that discordant shrieks from dozens of seabirds rent the air as they wheeled above fishing boats tied up at the town wharf, the sounds from the sawmill providing an obbligato. Cars and light trucks from the south came in ones and twos, but those from the north came in gaggles of ten or so as they were disgorged by the ferry. At about afternoon tea time the service cars returned, stopped briefly, then roared away up the gravelled slope of the Highway towards Moruya. There always were some cars in town with the distinctive F.C.T. (Federal Capital Territory) number plates pointing to drivers brave enough to tackle 90 miles of rough gravel road from Queanbeyan to Braidwood, then a drop of nearly 2000 feet via tortuous windings to another ferry over the Clyde River at Nelligen; before arriving at the main ferry at The Bay.

The weather throughout our wonderful holiday had been fine and we were all a little sad when on the last day Dad went into the sheoak swamp with Mum and me to obtain some staghorn plants growing high up in crotches of the sheoaks, to take back to Willoughby. Next day Overland was packed as for our trip down here and we made the distance back home in one big day.

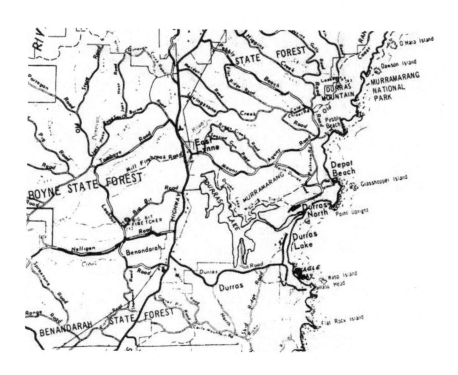

1933 - A BABY SISTER

With Dad and all of us nippers back to School, Dad resumed weekend trips to Mona Vale beach. On our return from one of these trips in March 1933, a thunderstorm came up as Overland was returning along High Street Willoughby, causing the shiny asphalt surface to become 'greasy' (Dad's term), and without warning, right opposite Robert Street, the car skidded and turned completely around, to face the opposite direction. The O.S. rear wheel slid off the asphalt onto the metalled road shoulder, where the tyre gripped, causing the car to turn over on its offside, and breaking three spokes in that wheel (the same as had been fitted in Lithgow in 1924). Acid pouring out from the battery, which was under the driver in Overland, added to Dad's discomfort. Mum related afterwards that she looked in the back to see all four of us 'tumbling about like cushions'. Actually no one was seriously hurt, and Dad's principal complaint was over the poor standard of repair done by Matheson's NRMA garage at North Sydney Station. They had replaced the broken spokes with new ones hand made from Australian hardwood, and a bit rough at that, Dad could have done a better job himself; this wheel always creaked afterwards when on the move. Uncle Robert Thompson passed away not long after, on March 16., aged only 47.

My snap of Mary with Mum, Willoughby 1935.

In May Dad drove us in Overland to Cullen Bullen for a holiday in the home of Mum's Aunty Ethel McGeachie (nee Scobie), whose husband Uncle Jim, was manager of the local coal mine, and were holidaying elsewhere. We kids enjoyed the private tennis court, unlimited use of electric radiators (free power from the mine), and tree ripened Granny Smith apples; one day Dad drove us out on the Highway to within sight of Bathurst, for a picnic; this was the furthest west we had ever been.

It was not until months later on 25th September 1933, at a private Hospital in High Street Willoughby, when Mum had presented us with a baby sister, that I realised that it was the second time that Mum had been involved in a motor accident whilst she was pregnant. We were very proud of our little sister, who had been named Mary Warren; brother Joe especially so, no more was he to be referred to as 'the baby'.

This dramatic change in the family circumstances filled Dad with serious reservations about going to a camp at Durras at the end of the year, but after many assurances from us bigger children that we would help Mum in looking after baby Mary, plus Mum actually looking forward to a holiday break, Dad relented and drove us again to Durras in Overland, pitching the tent and dining room in the same position as last year just behind the sand dunes. Camping rates had shot up by one shilling to three shillings and sixpence per week, there were still no 'facilities', but fresh milk now was available at Towns', where his sister in law, Mrs Kate Strawbridge, had come down permanently from Sydney, to help run the place, including milking several cows, and baking bread in the large wood fired oven in the old home of her childhood. Fishing was very good and we lived on them and rabbits. As part of the 'deal' with Dad, I became Mum's aide-de-camp for baby Mary, and became quite expert at crawling out on a fallen tree to obtain clean (but brackish) swamp water for washing the baby's clothes. Apart from this change, our camp routine of 'brunch' preceded by a dip in the surf was unchanged from last year.

A schoolteacher named Anderson camped with his wife and two daughters, Jean and Kit (actually Catherine) a couple of hundred yards away; my sister Nance became friendly with Kit, I with Jean.

Dad was not so friendly with a big family named Walker, from Ashfield, who for years had camped in the spot we had settled in, and had to find another spot 150 yards further north, needing to be cleared of fallen timber. I later became friendly with Charlie Walker, who was about my age.

There was a sadness early in January when Dad heard from Aunty 'Poll' that her daughter Gladys Esma Gow, had been killed in a motor accident at 'The Elbow' on Bulli Pass, on the first day of 1934, at the age of 27 years. She had been pillion passenger on a motor cycle being driven up the Pass by her fiance, when they were struck by a runaway 1919 Ford sedan driven by a Methodist Minister, the car's 4 wheel (mechanical) brakes had burned out on the steep descent; the driver thought that with good brakes it was safe to make the descent in top gear.

The weather was fine until the middle of January 1934 when a southeasterly gale sprang up and continued for five days without let up, bringing torrential rains to the whole of the South Coast. Durras received 24 inches in a 36 hour period, and many fallen trees cut the road and telephone line to Benandra; there were reports also of a bridge washed away. Our tent escaped the full force of the gale thanks to the protection of the adjacent sand dune, but a fully grown blackbutt tree 15 inches in diameter only 30 yards away from us was snapped like a carrot at 10 feet above ground. At the height of the gale, a piece of dead timber 4 feet long by 5 inches thick fell on the tent tearing a hole through the 'Birkmyre' to end up on Overland's O.S. front mudguard, allowing rain to pour in and drench the magneto ignition, making the car inoperative; to Dad's disgust. The two McMillan brothers, who were holidaying with their sister Kate, and no doubt had seen this sort of weather as boys, came down in their Buick tourer to help, and moved our family and bedding through floodwaters 18 inches deep, and up to an empty house near Towns'. Tremendous seas were whipped up by the gale and huge waves coupled with king tides meant that the floodwaters took days to go down - we kids had a wonderfully exciting time.

As soon as the weather cleared, Dad went back to our tent and stitched up the roof (he always carried needle and thread for canvas repairs), opened the sides to dry out the ignition, then by arrangement with Jack Towns, re-pitched the tent alongside a single roomed hut which stood empty, back from the beach. Dave and I helped him with this, also to rebuild the beds, but not the dining room; instead we used the hut which had an open fireplace, with its own corrugated iron chimney, and a rough table. Mum was kept very busy during all of these commotions, looking after Mary (then 4 months old) and the needs of the whole family.

Meanwhile it was confirmed that a bridge on the Benandra road had been washed out, which meant that Durras, including the camps at Durras Lake, was isolated, seriously affecting people who had to get back to work. So a working party was organised by the younger McMillan, Roy, who ran a sawmill at Wauchope. Dad of course volunteered and took me (13 years old) along to help. At the washaway we found that a single 25 foot span timber bridge had been lifted bodily by the floodwaters and deposited intact some 30 yards downstream. Moving it back was beyond the available equipment, so the men decided to build a temporary 15 foot span single lane bridge just above the water level in the creek. Several trees were felled to make girders and seatings, and a deck was provided by borrowing some planks from the damaged bridge. Dad's axe was in demand by the professional axemen, because it was the sharpest - he always kept it sharp, and in a leather protector - 'a sharp axe is safer than a blunt one' he would say to me. A small queue of anxious campers put the new structure into use immediately it was pronounced finished by Roy and Jack.

The next day back at our camp, I went down with an acute attack of measles, so severe that Dad gave thought to driving me to Milton Hospital, as Mum was almost overwhelmed by having Mary to look after as well as me. Fortunately Mrs. Bardsley, the wife of a lecturer from Newcastle Technical College in the larger cottage nearby, had been a Nurse in the first AIF, and she advised Mum that if I was kept in a darkened room my eyesight would not be damaged, and my recovery was sure. So the hut had the window blanked out with a grey blanket, and the door kept closed for over a week, during which my temperature soared to 104 degrees Fah. for three days. I did recover, and in time to see brother Joe succumb to the same disease, although not so severely.

Fishing for the remainder of our holiday was not good due to the continuing heavy ground swell, which Dad tried to counter by making a lot of double weight lead sinkers. Great quantities of seaweed were in the surf, making swimming unattractive, and tons of the stuff were dumped on the beaches at each high tide, and the smell of decaying seaweed was pervasive.

Then it was time to pack up, and on our way home to Willoughby, we became aware all through to Wollongong, of the extent to which many people had suffered in the gales and the torrential rain; the DMR was very busy on road repairs. It was almost a relief to be in the familiar surroundings of solid walls and roof, then it was back to School for all of us children except Mary. I went into 3rd Year at North Sydney Boys High, whilst brother Dave had made up his mind to do something connected with the land, so Dad was persuaded to let him enrol in 1st Year at Hurlstone Agricultural High School at Glenfield, which was a long daily trip by tram and train.

With the increase in the size of our family, Overland's capacity was being severely taxed, so not long after our return Dad decided to have a look at a new Ford tourer, on display in a dealer's showroom at Crows Nest, next to the Mater Hospital; I tagged along. Fitted with detachable wire wheels and fatter tyres, it was roomy and smart; Dad was attracted by its battery and coil ignition - more reliable in wet weather than Overland's magneto. The salesman went into raptures over the optional V8 engine, which he assured Dad, although more powerful than the standard 4 cylinder job, would use no more petrol (who was he kidding?). Being much faster than our 'bus' (Dad's term for the Overland), the Ford was set a good deal lower; I saw him take a look under the new car, and I think that he decided it might have trouble with the bush tracks at Durras - we kept Overland.

As baby Mary was well able to walk before the end of 1934, Dad's preparations for the end of year camp became less tentative, and Mum was keen for a holiday, so as soon as School 'broke up' Overland was packed as before, with the addition of an extra roll up mattress/bed for Mary. With the improvements being made to the Highway by the DMR we could make the trip in one big day, and once more pitched the tent alongside, and south of the one roomed hut. This was convenient for cooking with its sheltered fireplace, and its own rainwater tank. Mary of course was keen to make use of her new found mobility to explore this interesting place, hence Dad had to erect a wire netting fence three feet high to enclose the front of the tent. The rest of the family had to remember this obstacle in the dark - some of the younger ones did forget.

Fishing had not recovered from last year's storms, but Dad persisted with various rigs, and we were seldom without; there always was 'squnce' to fall back upon, we had picked up a half cheese as usual at Yatte Yattah on the way down. Also Fred Jones, son-in-law of Mrs E.Thomsen who owned the main store in 'The Bay', had started deliveries to Durras of groceries and vegetables in a new Dodge one ton truck, with a proper canopy; it was very convenient; bread and milk we still obtained from Mrs. Strawbridge.

While we were still at Durras, the *Sydney Morning Herald* carried the results of the Intermediate Exams; I had been successful, and on our return home, Dad gave me a 'reward' of thirty shillings. With this I was able to fulfil an ambition of owning a movie camera, a *Pathe Baby* hand cranked machine, which took 9.5 mm width film in 30 foot cassettes; which I purchased at Heiron and Smith's billiard store in Elizabeth Street, Sydney. I made a pan/tilt head out of scrap steel, and Dad provided the folding legs out of Queensland maple, neatly sawn, planed and french polished, during the year.

The year 1935 passed with the other main event in Sydney being the non-appearance of the Messiah anywhere, following which the owners of the reserved seats in the Amphitheatre at Balmoral Beach made haste to have their brass nameplates removed. The Theosophists' credibility was in tatters, Dad's scepticism was justified.

1936

During 1935 Dad lived and planned for the next Durras camp, and come school 'breakup' in December, was ready to pack Overland, and head south to our usual spot for pitching of the tent alongside the one roomed hut. Jack Towns had allowed Dad to store a lot of our heavier camp gear in a barn opposite Towns' house, so it was not long before Dave and I helped Dad get everything 'ship shape' for the 5 week stay. We did put up the wire netting fence for 'little sister control', but she soon found ways of getting over it, or of crawling under the tent walls; the fence was removed, we just had to 'keep our eyes peeled' in her direction.

Rabbits that year were scarce, but fishing was very good, and of course there was an occasional change of diet with Dad's 'squnce,' made with the usual a mixture of some Yatte Yattah cheese; the Andersons again were camped on the flat, and Nance and Kit kept each other company going up to Mrs. Strawbridge for milk and bread.

Durras' charms had been extolled by Mum to an old friend of the Roberts, Mr. Streatfield who recently had been widowed. He came down the same day we did, in his olive green 1929 Desoto sedan, driven by his son Bert, and daughter-in-law Mace. Mr. Streatfield who was elderly had never before camped in his life, but fitted in quickly and soon stopped wearing a tie. I introduced him to fishing at Mill Point where he became ecstatic at catching his very first fish; Bert's distinctive shriek of laughter closely resembled his father's. By this camp, Dad had taken to travelling further afield to Flat Rock, where fishing was better, but the descent of the cliff face (in retrospect) was quite dangerous - Mace was appalled at the way we kids, especially Mary, would go up and down without supervision.

While we were in this camp, the momentous news came of the death in London on 20th January, of King George V. Dad explained to us that the official announcement of 'The King is dead. Long live the King', meant that the King's eldest son automatically became the monarch, and would be known as Edward VIII.

After our holiday had ended and we were home in Willoughby, Dad received news of the death of his elder brother William Thompson, in Cessnock on 9th February; such was the size of Dad's family we never had met him.

Out at Morrison's farm at Castle Hill Aunty Nance and Uncle Sandy, exhausted by the never ending work of their 1200 poultry, allowed themselves to be charmed by a plausible youngish fellow named Osborne into handing over their entire farm on payment of a small deposit. This fellow came from an 'upper crust' family in Potts Point, and knew nothing about farm work, or it seemed to us, **any** sort of work. The Morrison's failure even to talk to a solicitor caused Dad to remark to Mum that 'they must have been work silly' to have permitted such an arrangement.

It was this year on 7th March, that alarm bells sounded even here in Australia of dire things to come, when the German dictator, Adolf Hitler, marched his troops into the de-militarized zone of the Rhineland, as an Army of Occupation; Uncle Sandy and Dad had long discussions on the matter - neither France nor Britain had been able to do other than protest.

Dad's family received another loss on 24th November 1936 when his sister Jane (Aunty Jinny) died in Hamilton, at the age of 67 years - our cousin Edna now was alone.

After leaving the Castle Hill farm, Morrisons lodged temporarily in a cottage in Castle Hill Road opposite Victoria Road, then moved into a fairly new fibro tiled roof cottage on a couple of acres of undeveloped land at the corner of New Line Road and a lane (since widened and named Valda Street). There was a 35 foot gum tree near the house, and Dad could see that its lean towards the house was a danger in high winds, so one hot summer day he and Uncle Sandy attached a long rope to a point on the trunk about 15 feet from the ground, and the other end to Morrison's 'new' Austin 1928 tourer. This was in preference to Overland because it was a good deal heavier and had a 4 speed gearbox. Uncle Sandy kept the engine running and 'rode' the clutch to hold the rope taut, whilst Dad cut the tree roots on the side facing the house. Before long Austin was able to pull the tree over, and it came crashing down, its top leaves just brushing the car.

Later that day Dad set to work at the back of the block down by the little dry creek, to fell a dead tree for firewood for his sister's kitchen stove. He had just completed the second 'scarf' (his term) in the 12 inch diameter trunk, and had stepped back to allow the tree to fall away from him, when a 6 foot length of dead wood dislodged by the vibrations from the very top of the tree, plunged into the ground between his feet, clipping the end of his nose on the way - there was blood everywhere; I was safe enough at 20 feet away where he had told me to stand. Back in the house for bandaging, and a cup of tea from Aunty Nance, he observed that 'it had been a close shave'.

Before the end of 1936, Edward VIII who had been living with his mistress, a twice-divorced American woman named Wallis Simpson, abdicated when the British Government under Prime Minister Stanley Baldwin, flatly refused to accept her as Queen. Uncle Sandy was pleased, especially as the successor as George VI, already was married to a Scotswoman; Dad agreed.

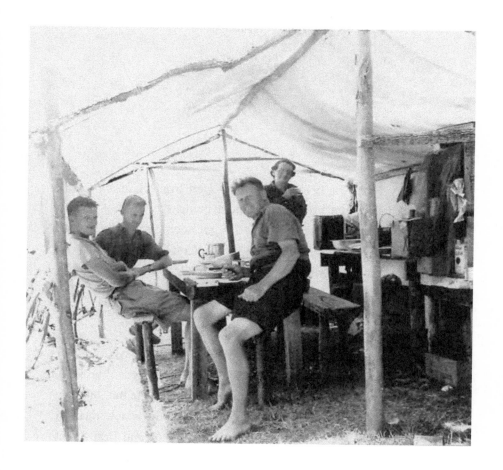

Geoff, Bob Roberts, Dad and Mum in our tent at Durras. Photo Alan Roberts.

1937

The many events of 1936 did not deter Dad from planning for the next Durras camp, the principal problem being space - not only in Over-land but also in the camp itself. He got over the first by making use of the freight service of the I.&S.C.S.N. Company to send heavy camp gear from their wharf in Sussex Street, Sydney, where the *S.S.Bergalia* usually berthed, to the town wharf in Batemans Bay, sending our stuff down early in December. Then he bought a new cottage tent, 10 feet by 8 feet, complete with fly.

With these arrangements made Dad was able to fit all five of us plus Mum and himself into Overland and set out as soon as School broke up for Durras, where the new tent was pitched in front of the hut, but clear of the window, so as not to obstruct Mum's view of the beach; the OSE tent was pitched in the same place as last year. Mace and Bert Streatfield again came down, this time with his Uncle, who rode the distance on a motorcycle; they camped on the other side of the road amongst some blackberry bushes. This year our Cameron cousins Lin, Bob and Doug came down with Uncle Bill and Aunty Mu in their 1932 Studebaker sedan; they camped 100 yards from us on our side of the road.

Fishing was very good, but rabbits were hard to find. On my return from an unproductive expedition, I started emptying the Browning 0.22 rifle in the hut, taking 12 cartridges out of the magazine, then pointed the muzzle upwards, pressed the trigger believing it empty, and a neat hole appeared in the iron roof - Dad came racing in, but no one was hurt; I had forgotten the 13th cartridge in the breech; lesson learned - always count your cartridges; that was handy later in the Army.

The weather continued warm to hot, and on one hot windy day, coals from Streatfield's fireplace got into the dry blackberry bushes, and suddenly there was a big blaze which threatened their camp and their brand new 1936 Vauxhall 14 H.P. single seater. Only strenuous efforts by Dad and Bert, and some other campers, saved the car and tent. Altogether it had been an eventful camp, during which also I had received notice in *Sydney Morning Herald* of my pass in the Leaving Certificate.

Back home after our holiday, in April, and thanks to some lobbying by Dad's Soccer friend, Mr. Arthur Willetts, who was the Head Messenger at the Sydney Water Board, I started work with the Board at the Construction Office in Hale Street Botany, as a Junior Professional, at 25 shillings per week, and very interesting work too.

This relieved my parents of some financial strain, and encouraged Dad to think about a more up-to-date car, for, in addition to Uncle Sandy's Austin, and Streatfield's Vauxhall, Uncle Bob had traded in his Ford single seater for a new 1936 Ford V8 sedan. Dad looked around and found a smart 1929 Chrysler Plymouth tourer at Hendersons Motor Sales, North Sydney, and with the help of a loan from Aunty Alice, traded in Overland. We all felt the loss of a faithful go anywhere servant, but the 'new' car was more roomy and comfortable, as well as being faster, especially on hills - it had a high ratio 2nd gear; and with four wheel hydraulic brakes it was much better able to stop. To me on Saturday 9th October 1937, Overland looked forlorn at the kerbside in Berry Street, as Dad drove us away in the Plymouth; we never saw Overland again.

By the winter of 1937 the situation at Morrison's farm at Castle Hill had seriously deteriorated, Mr. Osborne was not looking after the poultry, and had not made even one payment to Uncle Sandy, who eventually had to take drastic legal action to repossess the farm. Dad's involvement in this was only peripheral, and advisory.

Durras 1938, Mum and Dad.

(Top) JW Thompson's 1928-29 Plymouth outside the YatteYattah
Cheese Factory, en route to Durras 23 December 1937; (lower)
The Thompson camp at Durras 1934.

1938

Dad as usual planned ahead for the next camp at Durras, and once more sent down heavy gear via *S.S.Bergalia*. We got away in the Plymouth just before Christmas. I managed to obtain a few days leave from the Water Board Construction office at Malabar where I had been instructed in driving and gained my licence on 26th November. This was to be the last camp in which the whole family, including me, travelled together. Dad took it quietly in the unfamiliar vehicle, and we stayed overnight at 'Gascoyne', the dairy farm at Cambewarra owned by Alec and Judy Brown, whom we had met in Nowra on our first trip south. There was a lot to see around the farm, and we found their four boys good company. Next day, as on previous occasions, we stopped at Yatte Yattah Cheese Factory for a half cheese. All of the family went in to 'help' - I stayed on the side of the gravelled Highway, and took the first photo of Plymouth with a new mini camera which my sister Nan had received as a present. On to Durras where improvements had been made to the road in from the Highway; we lost no time in pitching the two tents alongside the hut, and started enjoying the fine warm weather and beach; Dad, Dave and Joe got going on fishing immediately - I had only a few days, being now a 'worker', and soon had to return via service car (7 seater Studebaker) from Benandra to Bomaderry, thence in the green painted Daylight Express to Central, and Willoughby. The family stayed on until the end of January.

Not long afterwards, the Morrisons were able to return to their farm, which they found in a real mess. They called in a builder to make some repairs, also some alterations for greater comfort in winter-time; Dad as before became involved in fixing things up for his sister. Dad and Uncle Sandy had plenty of politics to talk about when on 12th March 1938 Hitler marched his troops into Austria (his old homeland), and annexed the whole of Austria to Germany; war with Germany for the second time, now seemed certain.

In July Mum decided that my four nights per week of lectures in the Local Government Engineering Diploma Course at Sydney Techni-cal College, were turning me into a social recluse. So, without telling me anything, she booked me on my 'night off' for 3 months tuition in Ballroom Dancing, at Lindfield, and paid in advance. My objections to using up my only 'spare' night had been partially overruled - I still had a last defence - how was I to get to Lindfield? 'Easily', said Mum, 'your father will lend you the car'. I had been outmanouvered! The lessons were given in the Masonic Hall, and led by a Miss Edna Mann, assisted by two men and three women 'tutors'; I felt awkward, especially on the slippery floor; how was I going to endure this? The question evapo-rated on the second night of the lessons, when, 20 minutes in, I caught sight of this dainty creature, dressed in forest green, come in a bit late, and wend her way very carefully across the polished floor; she had a turned up nose in the midst of peaches and cream complexion, with wavy brown hair down to her shoulders; I determined at once to get to know **her**. This I did, although there was a bit of competition, and I was more than pleased to find that her voice matched the rest; her name was Evelyn Storey and she came from Hornsby, but worked as a Chil-dren's Nurse in a private home in Killara; she had only come to these classes in place of a girl friend, who had paid in advance, but had had to drop out.

In August-September School holidays, Dad drove the family in the Plymouth to stay for two weeks in a rented cottage at Blackheath, just off the Hat Hill Road; I managed to fit in a few days from my job in the Water Board, by then in Head Office. There was a tennis court next to the house, and as the weather was crisp and fine, we kids spent a lot of time making it useable. Dad took us all on picnic trips, including one to the Megalong Valley, and another much longer, with me 'at the wheel' for the first time in this car, past the entrance to Jenolan Caves, up a very steep hill (my first experience of 'serious' first gear) through to Oberon, hoping to make Kanangra Walls. However recent snowfalls had made the track risky, so we stopped for lunch in the bush (Mum complained that I 'always take movies when we are eating' when I set up the tripod for my camera); we went home via Bathurst. On another trip Dad drove us to the fabled Mudgee, where we all had a good look (from the street) at my childhood home ('Kildallen' at 76 Court Street). Dad was becoming quite enthusiastic about his speedy Plymouth (it cruised comfortably at 45 mph.) and in between other trips dashed down to Sydney one day to see an International Soccer match against India. My school friend Jim Clark came up for a couple of days, and together we took train to Newnes Junction, whence we walked the length of the abandoned Zig Zag railway formation down to Lithgow. The old Clarence tunnel had us beat though, we'd forgotten to bring torch and neither had matches, so we had to walk over the top through the bush; the sight of this spectacular engineering feat made it worthwhile.

Following the annexation of Austria by Hitler last March, Dad and Uncle Sandy in their political discussions (by now back in the old farm at Castle hill), were agreed that the international situation now looked ominous. The British Government evidently thought so too, and while we were holidaying at Blackheath, their PM Neville Chamberlain had attempted to ward off a war with Germany by signing an Agreement with Hitler at Munich, which had included Hitler's 'reasonable demands' that Czechoslovakia cede to Germany **all** those districts of Bohemia and Moravia which contained 50% or more of German speaking people - there was not much left! Chamberlain returned to England proudly waving this piece of paper, announcing that it was 'Peace in our time'. No one was really convinced, certainly neither Uncle Sandy nor Dad.

Their unease was justified two months later in November, when Hitler showed his contempt for Britain and the rest of Europe, and his hatred of Jews, by sending his thugs (in uniform) to smash the windows of thousands of stores and businesses owned by Jewish people through-out Germany. Such was the heap of smashed glass that the night became known as 'Kristallnacht'. Also that night, Synagogues were set on fire by these thugs, and books by Jewish authors publicly burned in huge bonfires. I wondered where this was going to end; also why did Dad dislike Jews? (It was not until half a century later that it dawned upon me that this probably came from Dad's upbringing in that part of the Church of England which shared the then doctrine of the Roman Catholics that God had 'finished with the Jews').

School football Premiers 1939, detail shows Dad (coach North Sydney Public School) with son Joe (top).

1939

On 16th December 1938 Dad drove all of the family (except me) in Plymouth to camp in two tents at the usual 'spot' alongside the one roomed hut at Durras. I travelled down later with Mr. and Mrs. Seccombe, parents of Norma, a friend of my sister Nance; they lived at 210 Eastern Valley Way, and owned a new navy blue Hillman with a 10 horsepower engine, Mr. Seccombe continually had to be changing gears; but it **was** very quiet and comfortable.

I was still attached to the Construction Section in the Water Board Head Office under Mr. W.Hudson (later to become Commissioner of the Snowy Hydro Electric Scheme) hence my stay at the camp was short and I missed the 'Black Friday' in the second week of January when disastrous bushfires raged all the way down from west of Sydney into North Eastern Victoria. Dad and the family, plus the Camerons who were also camped at Durras that year, spent the sweltering day in the cool of the cave at the northern end of the main beach, near where the village now stands.

My dancing classes had terminated in October 1938 with a formal dance at the Hall (now a Theatre) in Marian Street Killara, at which I had arranged to meet Eve. Dad lent me the Plymouth to be able to

Dad, Joe Thompson with his 25lb. Blue groper and Dave Thompson at Flat Rock. Photo Alan Roberts

drive her home, only to find that Burt's home, where she worked, was only one block away from the Hall. From then on I kept in touch by visiting her at Burt's. Dad was a bit dashed when I informed him that Eve was **not** the daughter of an old Soccer friend of his, Mr. Sid Storey who was State M.P. for Hornsby, nevertheless he lent me the Plymouth to take her for a picnic to the Upper Colo River area on 5th February 1939, together with Dave, Nance and Joe. We picked Eve up at Montview Parade Hornsby Heights, and I took some movies with my hand cranked camera. Only a few days later, Dad's brother-in-law Sid Gow died, and Dad drove himself to Wollongong next day for the funeral.

On 15th March, Hitler gave clear notice of his intentions by marching his troops into the residue of Czechoslovakia, which included the massive SKODA armaments works there; Hitler issued a decree making the newly seized territory 'a protectorate of the Reich'.

About this time we became aware that our next door neighbour in No. 100 (now 200 following the bridging of Sugarloaf Creek to connect the two sections of Lyle Street) Mr. Thias, who came from western Germany, and had never been naturalized, was being visited on some Saturday afternoons by crafty looking men, in pairs, who seemed to me (they spoke only in German) to be trying to persuade Mr. Thias to 'return to the Fatherland', a notion which he was firmly resisting. Mrs. Thias who came from the northern (German speaking) part of Switzerland, refused even to speak to these men, nor would their Australian born daughters Heidi and Mignon. When after declaration of war in September, there was a general round up of non-naturalised aliens, Dad was approached by Australian Security Officers, and was able to inform them of Mr. Thias' determined non-cooperation with the Nazis. Coming from an ex RAN officer, this no doubt had a good deal to do with Mr. Thias avoiding internment; indeed he eventually was accepted into the Civil Construction Corps, and served in the Northern Territory.

As it was now evident to my parents that I was not going to 'drop' Eve, they invited her to our place one Sunday for dinner, which was, as usual, a roast, and served on the big cedar table on the back verandah, now become our dining room following extensive work by builder Alec Flew, to replace the centre post by a pair of sloping timber struts, and four sliding glass windows. Three of my family already had met Eve on the Colo picnic, and I was interested to observe Dad's reaction - he **must** have been impressed to judge by the number of jokes he was cracking as he carved the roast at the end of the table!

Hitler's armies invaded Poland early in September 1939, and Britain declared war in support of its treaty with that country. Immediately, also because of treaties, our PM Mr. Menzies, came on the radio to announce that it was his 'melancholy duty' to inform his fellow Australians that we were at war with Germany.

Notwithstanding this, and the rapid raising by the Commonwealth Government of a Second Australian Imperial Force to serve overseas, Dad decided once again to plan for a Durras camp, and as the 'OSE' tent was starting to show signs of age, ordered a new, and bigger (24 by 15 foot) marquee tent from Crows Nest tentmaker D. Hardie. This also was to have a Birkmyre roof, but because of the extra length, needed two centre poles; complete with ropes, poles and pegs, the price was to be £44. with the 'OSE' as trade-in.

Durras 1940. Back Row: Geoff, Bob Roberts, Dad and Mum- Joe and Marj Thompson, Dave. Seated: Nan, Joe, Mary and Frisky/Whisky the dog. Photo Alan Roberts

1940

The new tent was ready by the end of November 1939, and Dad and I took delivery of it in the Plymouth. A fortnight later after School broke up, he and Mum packed up and set off with the family (except me) for a new camp site at Durras, further south from the hut, on level ground about ¼ mile north of the old sawmill, and sheltered by a low timbered hill from southerly gales - Dad always was touchy about them. I came down later by train and service car to Benandra, for a short stay. The weather and the fishing were good, but the war was starting to over-shadow everything; and family changes were afoot - Dad was about to be transferred to the Staff of Sydney Technical High School, Dave was looking for a farm job, and in February I was transferred to the Water-mains Extensions Branch in Head Office.

I went to my new job by tram over the Bridge, and was surprised one morning in April to see three large ships in the Harbour, which had arrived unannounced, and without any mention at all in either press or radio. However the 'grapevine' soon told us that they were the ocean liners 'Queen Mary' (brand new in grey paint, and huge) and 'Maure-tania' and 'Aquitania', which were old but very big. From the same source we also learned that all had been sent to Australia to be refitted as troopships, by the men from Cockatoo Island Dockyard. 'Queen Mary', 80,774 tons with a length of 1019 feet was too large to tie up at any of Sydney's wharves, and was anchored in Athol Bight, where lighters carried men and materials to her side. The other two vessels were able to be accommodated at Woolloomooloo finger wharf, where the workmen had direct access. Dad of course was most interested in this maritime activity from his new vantage point of a tram, as he too went across the Bridge to his new School...

Following Germany's invasion of Poland just before the northern winter in 1939, there came a period of stalemate, sometimes referred to as 'the phoney war', during which military activity was more than matched by the torrent of abusive propaganda from Germany's Dr. Goebbels. France had mobilized its Armed Forces and manned the Maginot Line of forts on its eastern borders facing Germany. Unfortunately the French never had completed the Maginot Line to the north, in the belief that the Ardennes Mountains would be a sufficient obstacle to armoured forces, hence were only lightly defended. On 10th May 1940, German mechanised forces including heavy armour, (using tactics devised in 1918 by Australian General Monash, by which they had been defeated) crashed through the Ardennes, and attacked the Netherlands, Belgium and Luxembourg. The British Government sent an Expeditionary Force of 10 Divisions (only **one** of which was mech-anised) and all the air cover they had, but it was not enough. The French Army, deficient in armour and aircraft, and had, but it was not enough.

The bulk of the British Army (about 250,000 men) retreated to the French Channel Coast, where they were rescued from the Dunkirk beaches by an unofficial armada of privately owned water craft of all descriptions, from southern England. The sudden onset of a few days of unexpected and unseasonably bad weather grounded the German

Air Force, thus giving protection to these small unarmed boats; Divine intervention was credited, in the circumstances even Dad gave that credence.

The whole Western European world, which of course included Australia, was in a state of profound shock and alarm, and no doubt the stress had some effect on Dad's sister Aunty Nance, who suffered a massive heart attack while peeling potatoes at the Castle Hill farm, and died on 15th June 1940. Dad attended another family funeral.

Only a week later on 22nd June, Marshal Petain who had succeeded M. Reynaud as France's Prime Minister, sought an Armistice with Germany, and this was signed in the presence of Hitler in the Forest of Compiegne, in the very same railway carriage in which the 1918 Armistice with Germany had been signed - Hitler made sure of that! I was visiting Eve at Burt's home that evening and decided to enlist in the Army as soon as I had finished the third year of my engineering studies at the end of the year. Petrol rationing at the rate of 4 gallons per month for private vehicles was imposed by the Commonwealth Government on 15th August; a few days before this took effect, Dad lent me the Plymouth to take Eve on a 'farewell picnic' to Kurrajong Heights, it rained steadily the whole trip.

With the death of Aunty Nance, it was more than ever necessary for Uncle Sandy to sell the farm, and a new buyer suddenly appeared 'out of the blue' - he was a Jewish man named Lowry who had managed with his family to escape from Germany about the time of the 1938 persecutions, and had just enough money to buy the farm. He was a big likeable fair haired man in his early fifties, had no experience in farm work and ill suited to it, **but** he was willing, and keen to make a new start, in Australia; so the sale went through, **with** legal advice this time, to Dad's relief. Uncle Sandy moved to a cottage at Narrabeen, near the tram terminus.

It was during 1940 that Dad started complaining about indigestion, and went for advice to our Doctor Lang, at the corner of Penshurst and

Forsyth Streets. He prescribed antacid tablets, and Dad went off roast and fried meals - Mum started grilling all his meat - this gave Dad some relief, and he was feeling well enough to plan for a trip to Durras at the end of the year, the prime consideration being saving enough petrol in drums to get there and back.

Dave had started work with a dairy farmer near Mullumbimby, but after months of 7 day a week duties, decided that he would like a change, and applied for a job in Tenterfield with a beekeeper named Sommerlad. While our parents were debating whether to allow Dave to go there, a murder took place in the Tenterfield district, involving a person with that name. I remember them talking about a letter which they had received from Mr. Phil Sommerlad, Dave's prospective employed, assuring them of his personal integrity, and non involvement in the murder case.

Dave was back at Willoughby by now, and we decided to get to the Durras camp independently, so put our bicycles on the South Coast Daylight Express ahead of Dad in the Plymouth. That afternoon we pedalled from Bomaderry to Ulladulla where we found a 'bed and breakfast' run by an elderly couple named Gresty, the charge was three shillings and sixpence each, and the breakfast of bacon and duck eggs was substantial. The Prince's Highway had been sealed to Benandra so we arrived at the camp site as last year before the family in the car, so were able to help Dad erect the tent etc.

Uncle Bill Cameron and his family came down later and camped near us, and not long afterwards Uncle Bob Roberts visited us in his 1936 Ford V8 sedan, bringing with him Uncle Alan who was on holidays from Melbourne. The weather and fishing were good, Dad caught a large groper off Flat Rock; both families used a boat launched from a little beach near the old sawmill for productive fishing, and Uncle Bob made a big fish trap, which must have attracted a large fish, it went berserk and wrecked the trap. Dave shot a swamp wallaby in Cook's Flat, and found that it had a live 'joey' in her pouch, so he was kept busy looking after this 'baby'. Uncle Alan was a keen photographer, both still with a 'Rolleicord' camera, and 9.5 mm movies, and both remain the best we have.

It was a great family camp, but the war was overshadowing everything, and I had determined to enlist early in 1941, so after Christmas Dad tied my bicycle on to Plymouth's luggage carrier, and drove me and the family across the Nelligen ferry, and up the mighty Clyde Mountain to Braidwood. Mum gave me a 'farewell picnic' just outside the Show-ground, then off I went to Bungendore (it rained the last 10 miles), Dad took the family back to Durras. I was dried out at the Royal Hotel, and next day went to Queanbeyan and Canberra, and overnight at the Collector Hotel (surrounded by bushranger memorabilia) then picked up a train at Goulburn for Sydney and home, on Saturday 31st December 1940. On the following Monday 2nd January I enlisted in the 2nd Field Survey Company, R.A.E., at their H.Q. in Strathfield, for training in Army mapmaking, in preparation for transfer to the A.I.F. Unit overseas in the Middle East. After the holiday at Durras, Dave went to Tenterfield to start work with beekeeper Mr. Sommerlad, where Dave started to be addressed by all as David.

(Top) Geoff in the Mains Section 1940 ; (lower) 1943. A.I.F. Survey unit, Geoff Thompson standing, far left

1941

The Army immediately put me on a 3 ton truck headed for New-castle, where I was changed into a 15 cwt. utility, which took me (and others) on to Grafton, where a Field Survey party was engaged on trig-onometrical surveying of a chain of intervisible mountain tops con-necting New South Wales and Queensland. This continued for some months, then I was transferred to topographical detail work, firstly at Scone, later over the Barrington Tops.

While I was there, vacancies occurred in the A.I.F. Unit in the Middle East, and another member of 2nd Company, Mark Stannard, and I were accepted. Eve and I decided to become engaged, and being a few weeks short of 21 years of age, Dad needed to be consulted - he could not see the sense of the idea, but agreed, reluctantly. I then made a quick train trip to farewell Dave in Tenterfield, and on my return, enlisted with Mark in the A.I.F. on 4th November, whereupon we were both promptly put on the overnight train to Melbourne. Mum it appeared, had rung Uncle Alan about me, and he was waiting for us at Spencer Street Station, where his enquiries nearly got him into serious trouble; Army troop movements were supposed to be secret.

HQ of 3rd Field Survey Company (Militia) at Woodend north of Melbourne was the assembly point for us and the 23 other A.I.F. reinforcements, who were coming from Queensland and other parts of Victoria, whilst waiting for the next troopship for the Middle East. Things changed dramatically on 8th December (7th in U.S.A.) when a powerful Japanese air attack took place against the American Naval Base at Pearl Harbour in the Hawaiian Islands, without any warning, and inflicting massive damage. Shortly afterwards Japanese ground forces attacked the Phillippines, where they came up against American troops under General Macarthur, also the Malayan Peninsular, where British troops and the Australian 8th Division immediately were involved. Our Government in Canberra demanded that the British High Command release all of our troops who were in the Middle East as soon as practicable; suddenly they did not need **us** as reinforcements, and we were sent out to various training Units in Victoria.

Family in the garden at 202 Eastern Valley Way (102 Lyle Street before 1939);
Back row: Geoff, Lin Cameron; Sitting left to right: Doug Cameron, Bob Cameron,
Joe, Dave (with Durras Joey), Kit Anderson, Mary, Nance and Jean Anderson

1942

Before long the whole of Malaya was in the hands of Japanese forces, and this meant the loss of most of our 8th Division; it was now evident that Australian cities were likely to be in the firing line, so Dad dug (I helped him when on a few days' leave) an air raid shelter in the backyard of our Willoughby home, next to the back fence; he then fitted it out. The stress of these days told on Grandma Roberts, who suffered a stroke on 5th February, and died three weeks later on 27th. On 19th February the same Japanese Task force which had been at Pearl Harbour, attacked Darwin in a savage morning raid, which inflicted great damage due to inadequacies in the warning system; there was a second raid that afternoon, nearly as effective. These raids continued for the next 18 months.

The Army finally sent most of us reinforcements to the 7th Field Survey Company (Militia) which had been in Darwin for nearly two years. The movement was by train to Alice Springs (3 days and 3 nights) followed by 3 days over 600 miles of exceedingly rough and dusty dirt roads to the southern end of the North Australia Railway, which took us in cattle trucks to Adelaide River, whence Army trucks took us up to the Unit camped at 18 miles south of Darwin.

Back in Sydney, Japanese submarines shelled Bondi, and midget types slipped past the boom at the Harbour entrance, and caused a lot of damage to small Naval vessels and casualties. By this time Eve had left Burt's, and had taken a clerical job at Nestles Chocolate Factory at Abbotsford, and lodged with a W.W.1 widow at Mons Street, Fivedock; Dad started making lots of wooden toys for children of servicemen from the Willoughby district. As Darwin was under more or less continuous Japanese attack, all letters to and from this area were censored, and I had to get used to my letters to Eve and home being censored by an Officer who was an old High School mate of mine. We A.I.F. reinforcements found that the Militia Unit to which we had been attached was, together with all other troops in Darwin, regarded by our Government in Canberra as being on Active Service, by reason of being stationed north of the most southerly Japanese air attacks, which had been at Katherine.

Dad and Mum were getting used to the idea of having a daughter-in-law, and kept in contact with Eve; she saw better opportunities elsewhere than at Nestles, and moved to a clerical job in Yates Seeds Warehouse in Sussex Street; here her supervisor was Miss Florence Ballhausen, who became a lifelong friend. My time in the Northern Territory came to an end with arrival of a relief Company, and our departure from the Adelaide River Railway Station on 13th April 1943; by this time the Stuart Highway to Alice Springs had been sealed; the change was profound. Before leaving camp I had sent a somewhat preremptory telegram to Eve warning her to be ready to be married; this took place on 28th April, four days after my arrival at my parent's home, and two days after Dad and I had walked the Servicemen-filled streets of Sydney on the Anzac Day holiday on Monday 26th. My parents made our home available for a Reception following the Service at Willoughby Presbyterian Church, and we had a week's holiday at Lawson in the Blue Mountains, then moved into a series of flats, ending at 3 Clanwilliam Street Willoughby.

My Unit was stationed at Wallgrove Camp, and after a few weeks of being reformed (during which I was allowed overnight leave) was moved by train to the Atherton Tableland, above Cairns in North Queensland. We had several weeks of Control Surveys from Mareeba out to Dimbulah, then I was sent with a Detachment of 30 men back to Katherine in the Northern Territory, for more Control Surveys, this time for Aerial photography which had been taken by the Air Force of the Roper River area.

Back in Willoughby Eve found that she was pregnant, and decided that a more spacious flat was needed, so located a commodious place in an old home at 36 Findlay Avenue Roseville. Dad was very helpful in helping her move with the Plymouth, and in selecting good secondhand furniture (new stuff was unprocurable). Dad also took on extra teaching of Mathematics at Evening Classes at his old School, North Sydney Boys' High, as a replacement for a Teacher who had enlisted.

At the Roper River, the Wet Season started in the third week of October, and before long the Detachment had to move up to Darwin, in time, it so happened for the last sizeable Japanese air raid on 13th November. On the evening of 18th November (unbeknown to me of course) Dad had been delayed after the close of his lecture, by one of his students asking questions, to the extent that he only had a few minutes to catch the 9.15 pm 207 bus back to Willoughby. So Dad hurried out of the School into Tucker Street, and took a short cut through the backyard of North Sydney Hotel by jumping a fairly high fence, the sudden exertion brought on a massive coronary heart attack, and he collapsed outside the Hotel. Passersby called Police and an Ambulance, which took him to Royal North Shore Hospital, where the Medical staff gave him the best treatment known at the time, but he died some time after 10 pm. At home Mum had no idea of what had happened until about 11 pm when a policeman called at the front door and informed her that her husband had died suddenly.

As Dad was well known and respected in the Education and Soccer football community, his funeral was well attended, and many wreaths were sent. However being in Darwin, all communications were routinely delayed for security reasons, so Mum's letter did not get to me. In desperation more than a week after Dad's funeral, Mum went around to the Army Drill Hall in Tyneside Avenue a couple of blocks from our home, and managed to persuade them to let me know of Dad's death, through the Army's Signals system.

So at 4 pm. on 27th November it came like a 'bolt from the blue' in the Army's Larrakeyah Barracks in Darwin, for me to be summoned urgently to the nearby Signals Unit, and in the presence of several curious faces, to be handed a telephone through which Mum's tearful voice gave me the sad news; due to some technical problem, although I could hear her clearly, she could not hear me, a helpful woman telephonist at Alice Springs became the go-between to pass on what I had to say, which was not much, I was too shaken.

The Army moved quickly in granting me 7 days compassionate leave, and driving me 50 miles south to the Air Force Base at Coomallie Creek, where I boarded a RAAF C 47 (Dakota) courier plane to Brisbane; from there it was by overnight train to Sydney. Poor Mum was devastated by Dad's death and its suddenness, she was only 50½ years old; his passing was the end of an era for our family, nothing was ever to be the same again; we children were her consolation, together with the expected arrival late in January next, of a child for Eve and me.

My leave ran out quickly, and then it was the long train trip back to the Atherton Tableland where I arrived on my 23rd birthday, to be informed by the Army Railway Transport Officer that my unit had departed for Brisbane the day before (Ha! ha!). The Army held Christmas dinner for us in the transit camp at the foot of the rail descent from Atherton Tablelands, then it was back to Brisbane where in the Army camp at Grovelly I still was stationed when Eve and I were blessed on 31st January 1944 with the birth of a fine strapping (9 pound 2 ounces) baby boy. Due to travel restrictions I was unable to be present, but Eve and I over the phone, had agreed to call our baby boy Christopher. To our surprise Eve found that her cousin Bessie Gough (nee Hankin) had had a baby boy before us, and called him Christopher. All I could think of at Grovelly Camp was the name of an up market type Chevrolet car then called a Graham-Paige, so we called our son 'Graham', with 'Joseph' for his second name after the Grandfather he would never see. I am sure that Dad would have liked that.

Graham, Eve, Lesley and Mum at Parkes 1952.

Printed in Australia
AUOW01n1906020818
300990AU00002B/4

9 781925 706543